Transforming to a Networked Society

Transforming to a Networked Society

GUIDE FOR POLICY MAKERS

——

Nagy K. Hanna
Rene Summer

SRIBAN
BOOKS

Author royalties and a matching contribution from the publisher will go to the
Swedish Childhood Cancer Foundation (barncancerfonden.se)
Copyright © 2015 Nagy Hanna and Rene Summer
All rights reserved.
ISBN: 1942916000
ISBN 13: 9781942916000
Library of Congress Control Number: 2015901227
Sriban, Inc., 42 Beacon Hill Court, Gaithersburg, MD 20878-5401, USA

Contents

A Message from Ericsson

———

IF YOU ARE READING THIS in your office, take a look around. It's a safe bet that your colleagues, customers and working tools have all changed dramatically in recent years—and in one way or another, information and communications technology (ICT) is probably responsible.

More broadly, during the past couple of decades, ICT has become more evident in everyday life and in citizens' actions and behavior. ICT spurs economic development; it is positively correlated with GDP and growth, and therefore, it affects quality of life. When technology, as often is the case with ICT, is introduced at an individual level, it is primarily the social dimension that justifies individual efforts and willingness to adopt services more widely. The development of new skills and habits that follows greater use of technology will gradually be turned into more effective and productive practices across business and society.

Continued rapid technological development, driven by cloud-based services and more powerful mobile devices, sensors, big data, and analytics is set to accelerate the development ahead. In this emerging networked society, we are set to witness transformative change across all sectors of society. Change that will affect the way we live our daily lives, change that will affect the way business is conducted, and ultimately change to the cultural framework on which society is built.

Nations, economies, and societies that can realize the immense opportunities associated with ICT-enabled change and minimize associated risks will not only enhance national competitiveness and economic well-being of citizens but also make way for a sustainable change.

The societal capacity to manage such transformation in the most advantageous direction is of strategic significance and not without conflicting interests. Ultimately this capacity drives the long-term well-being of citizens by shaping the satisfaction of needs, the pace of social progress, and improvement in standard of living. Benefiting from transformational change requires sound and proactive public-policy making that shapes and determines the duration, cumulative strength, and sustainability of triple bottom-line benefits that can be achieved in the networked society.

Ericsson hopes that Nagy Hanna's writing will make a positive contribution and help policy makers around the world make important public policy choices and design appropriate policies, with the aim to maximize the socioeconomic benefits associated with the ongoing ICT-enabled transformation of countries at any level of development.

Patrik Regårdh

Head of Strategic Marketing, Ericsson

Foreword

———

THIS GUIDE FOR POLICY MAKERS and other stakeholders of e-transformation is a timely initiative, as countries at all levels of development are increasingly aspiring to use ICT for transformative and sustainable development. New waves of information and communications technologies and practices such as the mobile Internet, automated knowledge systems, cloud computing, big data, open data, analytics, and Internet of Things promise a further expanded toolkit for disruptive innovation and accelerated transformation.

The guide fills a key need: to provide a comprehensive and practical guide and sourcebook that speaks the language of development and addresses the needs of policy makers and strategists. It does a good job in bridging the gap between various ICT policy makers/specialists and their counterparts in various development sectors where ICT can play a transformative role. It should serve well the ICT for development community, development practitioners interested in leveraging ICT tools, and first and foremost, policy makers in developing countries and emerging markets. It provides tools, frameworks, and roadmaps for policy makers, their advisers, and development specialists to pursue their country's e-transformation journey. It helps the stakeholders of ICT-enabled transformation and country development strategists to collaborate and interact in ways that can creatively develop and implement national e-transformation strategies.

As a knowledge bank, the World Bank welcomes sharing knowledge in this nascent but critical area of development. The guide points to and draws on the Bank's literature and involvement in the ICT field.

I personally also wish to acknowledge the pioneering work of Nagy Hanna, who is both a leading thinker and practitioner of the ICT for development field, in the context of economic development. The guide draws on his long and extensive experience in this field, as well as his contributions to the literature and best practice.

The World Bank stands to help client countries at all levels of development in their e-transformation journey, through its financing, advice, knowledge sharing, mutual learning, and global networks and partnerships.

Randeep Sudan
Practice Manager (Global)
Information and Communication Technologies
Transport & ICT Global Practice
The World Bank

Objectives and Uses of the Guide

———

THIS IS A PRACTICAL, ACTION-ORIENTED policy guide targeted at high-level decision makers. Our aim is to make this guide available to local stakeholders and policy makers to facilitate their pursuit of transforming their economies and societies with the power of information and communications technology (ICT).

While developed economies have made huge ICT advances, the ICT revolution continues to sweep the world economy, and many ICT advances and disruptions such as cloud computing, big data/analytics, and the Internet of Things have yet to begin their most dramatic impacts. In fact, all economies and societies face expanding opportunities from ICT-driven innovation and transformation and are under stress from the dramatic pace of change and threats of this technological revolution.

The guide addresses diverse country audiences, reflecting the variety of country experiences at different levels of incomes and developmental learning. There is much to be shared between developed countries, emerging markets, and even the least developed countries. Countries at all levels of development are learning to master ICT-enabled transformation. Lessons to be shared cover both the fundamentals as well as new technologies where countries must be on a fast learning curve. Some developing countries are leapfrogging as in user-driven mobile innovation, mobile money, frugal innovation, and business-model innovation.

The guide's primary audience is policy makers in developed and developing countries. It can be used by aid agencies, financing institutions, and ICT multinationals that are increasingly engaged in assisting countries in their e-transformation journey with finance, partnership, and technical assistance. Researchers may find opportunities to contribute to this modest guide with tools, frameworks, and empirical evidence that are sorely lacking in this fast-changing field. In fact, the guide should be viewed as a living, evolving document that users and researchers can improve on over time.

The guide should help policy makers ask the right questions about the digitally fueled future, as much as it should point to the right directions or sources for answers. Policy makers, advisers, development agencies, e-leaders, and other stakeholders should ask themselves and their followers the hard questions. Many of the issues and choices arising from the ICT revolution pose dilemmas and uncertainties for which there are often no ready-made solutions or final answers. These dilemmas should be explored and managed over time. The specific answers for each country should come through invention, innovation, reimagination, experimentation, evaluation, and systematic learning. They should also come from dialogue and sharing among local stakeholders, and from the mobilization and adaptation of global knowledge in this fast changing field.

A more ambitious aim of this guide is to help change the way governments, development institutions, and financing agencies think about designing and investing in digital transformation so as to adopt a holistic-ecosystem view of the transformation process.

Nagy K. Hanna

Acknowledgments

―――

I WISH TO ACKNOWLEDGE THE help of several individuals and organizations. Rene Summer, director of government and industry relations of Ericsson, proposed the idea of this guide, secured Ericsson financial support, authored chapter 7 on policies, and gave valuable advice on the entire effort. Ericsson provided financial support for my writing without any strings attached. Our common aim is to raise awareness about the opportunities and challenges that policy makers face in their pursuit of transforming their economies and societies with the power of ICT.

I am also thankful for the helpful comments of colleagues at the World Bank: Randeep Sudan, Tim Kelly, and Samia Melhem.

I acknowledge the positive and thoughtful comments of Dr. Peter Knight, board member of Fernand Braudel Institute of World Economics; Dr. Nigel Cameron, president and CEO of the Center for Policy on Emerging Technologies; Lucienne Abrahams, director, LINK Centre, University of the Witwatersrand, South Africa; Dr. Sandor Boyson, research professor and codirector, Supply Chain Management Center, University of Maryland; Anil Srivastava, president, Open Health Systems Laboratory; Judith Hellerstein, CEO, Hellerstein & Associates; and Dr. James Spohrer, director, IBM University Programs and Cognitive Systems Institute.

I would also like to acknowledge the excellent editorial work of Shampa Srivastava.

Executive Summary

———

A NETWORKED SOCIETY IS A transformative augmentation of societies' capabilities to shape their physical, economic, social, and intellectual environments to their own ends with the power of digital networks. This transformation arises from the recent developments of ICT and its integration into economies and societies. It is a process of fundamental structural change, a shift to a new technoeconomic paradigm enabled by ICT.

WHY A HOLISTIC ICT-ENABLED TRANSFORMATION?

Mobile and digital technologies continue to evolve at a rapid pace as they expand into different societies and economies, generating a wealth of data from connections, sensors, and applications. The network no longer stands for mere connectivity. It is an important source for data-driven innovation, providing enormous potential to generate value for business and society. With drastic reduction in communication costs and easy access to powerful tools and platforms, we also have here a potent recipe for radical and disruptive innovation across industries, public services, and private life.

In tomorrow's networked society, most of the world's population will live in a culture of openness, sharing, and self-organization, fundamentally changing the way we engage, innovate, and collaborate. A powerful ICT "interaction infrastructure" will support the flow of information exchange and knowledge creation. The network will serve as a common-knowledge utility and a foundation for innovation and sustainable growth.

Digital transformation encourages evidence-based policy making, open and accountable institutions, partnerships, and collaborations, and inclusive innovation. It promises adaptive management of development programs via a rich variety of real-time feedback channels and agile, adaptive development processes.

MANAGING THE BENEFITS AND RISKS OF A REVOLUTION

As technological revolutions usher in profound social and institutional change, they also face resistance from established institutions and vested interests. Managing the social and institutional environment and its associated technoeconomic paradigm shift can involve painful adjustments and often the destruction of legacy systems, institutions, and processes. The ICT revolution can therefore require redesigning or building new networks of institutions, complete overhaul of regulatory frameworks and governance, new skills and competencies, and even radical changes to ideas and culture.

It is only when innovations are widely diffused and broadly adopted by people, businesses, and public institutions that any sustainable impact on economies and societies can be achieved. The institutional and public-policy frameworks prevailing in a society can assist—or constrain—this impact. This implies that policy makers' capacity to manage ICT-led transformation ultimately drives the well-being of nations. Policy makers must lead institutional change, empower change agents and innovators, and set policy frameworks for wide and effective adoption of new technologies. Sound public policy will shape and determine the duration, cumulative strength, distribution, and sustainability of socioeconomic benefits in the networked society.

ICT specialists tend to focus only on the benefits of the new technology, and not so much on the associated risks of job destruction, income inequality, and erosion of privacy and security. Policy makers therefore must address issues of transitional and long-term costs, such as the impact on job markets and skills, and on health, learning, and cognitive development, especially among children. These risks will increase as ICT and Internet-based applications penetrate farther into society. They will demand attention and resources and must be made an integral part of future ICT policy and e-transformation practice.

Although it may be beyond the competencies and mandate of specialized ICT ministries, managing these risks will allow a society to steer toward an inclusive and desirable vision of development. Reforms may be necessary in governance, in labor and tax policies, education, social policy, and welfare systems. Policy makers can be proactive in mobilizing government and society to address these issues. They cannot rely on technocratic solutions alone, or on their own narrow or outdated mandates, to meet these crosscutting challenges.

A STRATEGIC FRAMEWORK FOR DIGITAL TRANSFORMATION

To pursue coherent policies and reinforce ICT-enabled development initiatives, policy makers need a strategic framework. We see the digital-transformation ecosystem as composed of five interdependent elements:

i. ***Enabling policies and institutions.*** These constitute the environment that either enhances or obstructs interactions among all elements of e-transformation. They are critical in promoting the supply and use of ICT services in all sectors and are essential to fostering trust in a digital economy and networked society.

ii. ***Human capital.*** Skilled human resources are at the heart of the ICT revolution. Necessary skills include policy, technical, and change-management skills, as well as broad information and digital literacy, and technoentrepreneurship.

iii. ***ICT industry.*** A dynamic ICT ecosystem is necessary to adapt technology to local needs, manage and maintain technological infrastructure, develop local digital content and solutions, and effectively partner with global ICT suppliers. Local software development capability is a core competency.

iv. ***Communications infrastructure.*** This comprises affordable communications infrastructure, including access to the Internet, fixed and mobile narrowband and broadband, and other digital-connectivity tools.

v. ***ICT applications and institutional change.*** This includes ICT applications and complementary investments in institutional changes to transform key economic sectors.

This framework helps identify and mobilize key stakeholders. It maps the connections and relationships among diverse players concerned with e-transformation supply and demand. It facilitates the creation of a national consensus and promotes systematic thinking about ICT as an enabler of development. It also helps policy makers and stakeholders identify the missing links and constraints within the ecosystem that should be prioritized.

Nurturing a national ICT ecosystem

Interdependencies and scale effects play a critical role in ICT ecosystems. For example, broadband contributes to higher growth in countries with a critical mass of ICT adoption, reflecting return to scale. The impact of broadband on small and medium enterprises (SME) is likely to take a longer time to materialize, due to their slow accumulation of intangible capital and complementary capabilities. Conversely, the impact is higher when its adoption is combined with local incentives to innovate new applications. In short, the impact of broadband is neither automatic nor uniform across economies.

This reinforces the case for adopting a holistic, ecosystem-based approach. Policy makers need to design national ICT plans that go beyond information infrastructure investments and invest in other enablers of transformation. These include ICT education, ICT services development, policy reforms and institutional changes, ICT-led business process innovation, new business and organizational models, and e-leadership capabilities.

The process should start with an assessment of national e-readiness, benchmarking the country on key indices against comparable or leading nations. Appropriate benchmarking and e-readiness methodologies, despite their limitations, should spur national dialogue. A shared vision of the opportunities and challenges of the country's economy should guide the integration of ICT into a national development strategy. Such integration demands creative and intensive interactions between those immersed in the world of ICT and technological innovation, and those concerned with the goals and challenges of transformative development in specific contexts. It also requires sector leaders to view ICT as drivers of transformation in their sectors, rather than add-ons to their programs and strategies.

WHAT KIND OF TRANSFORMATION?

Transforming government. This guide illustrates a range of ICT applications to enable public-sector reforms across government, creating customer-centric transformation; sharing processes, infrastructures, and resources; developing integrated multichannels for service delivery with special emphasis on mobilizing demand for online services and monitoring their adoption and use. Mobile devices, open government data, big data, and analytics are promising and powerful tools for public sector transformation.

Transforming key service sectors. A vision-driven, reform-based strategy will be required for sustainable transformation. Integrated ICT strategies and investments must be synchronized with sectoral policies, regulations and investments. A sector transformation strategy will benefit from taking an ecosystem view of the target sector (demand), combined with a holistic view of the ICT ecosystem (supply). This view can be adopted for any service sector. The guide illustrates this for the education and financial sectors.

MASTERING THE DIGITAL TRANSFORMATION PROCESS

Leadership and institutional capabilities are two of the essential ingredients of digital transformation. Policy makers should define clear roles for government, private sectors, and other development partners in leading the transformation process. Leaders need to network and co-ordinate across institutions to set coherent policies, overcome political economy barriers, and manage structural changes. They should build institutions with the requisite core competencies to orchestrate and implement various elements of the transformation process. The guide outlines key design options for e-leadership institutions, the strengths and weaknesses of these options, and the core competencies required from transformational leaders.

Enabling policies and regulations are needed to harness ongoing technological changes and ensure their integration into the economy and society. Political and economic challenges will ultimately condition the focus and implementation of these reforms. Policy makers must focus on the key questions that a regulatory framework must answer, and the distinct regulatory approaches that will address digital transformation issues. An agile and coherent policy and regulatory framework is a key enabler of the digital transformation process.

A high-quality broadband infrastructure forms the foundation of a vibrant ecosystem. Universal access is key to serving unconnected populations, capturing scale and network effects, and building a truly inclusive and networked society. Policy makers must explore options for pursuing universal access, and adopt the right policies for managing the spectrum, which has become a critical resource for mobile-broadband networks.

THE LESSONS SO FAR

Based on data from countries that have experienced digital transformation, we have ten recommendations for policy makers:

i. Commit to a holistic, long-term transformation strategy that is integral to a national development strategy.

ii. Leverage stakeholder engagement and coalitions to build a shared vision and commitment for the goal of digital transformation.

iii. Tap synergies among actors in the e-transformation ecosystem, and exploit supply- and demand-side economies of scale.

iv. Attend to the soft infrastructure or local capacity to master digital transformation through leadership, policies, and institutions.

v. Pursue public-private partnerships to tap private sector innovation, resources, and know-how required for transformative change.

vi. Emphasize digital diffusion and inclusion for broad-based and equitable transformation.

vii. Adopt strategic approaches to funding to cover innovation, flexibility, coordination, and time horizon needed for all elements of digital transformation.

viii. Balance strategic direction with local initiative to generate a dynamic for national drive, local experimentation and adaptation, and fast scaling.

ix. Enable change, innovation, and learning via decentralization, knowledge sharing, innovation funds, and change-management processes.

x. Practice agile and participatory monitoring and evaluation from the start and throughout the transformation process.

These fundamentals can be mutually reinforcing. Practicing them should help countries and local governments build capacity to master the digital transformation process. It is our firm belief that mastering this process is likely to be the defining core competency of the twenty-first century.

Part One: The Big Picture

———

This first part of the guide is composed of two chapters. It paints the big picture concerning why countries pursue digital-transformation strategies and why a holistic approach to transformation is the most effective. It conceptualizes a new way of thinking about the roles of ICT for development: holistic and transformative. It outlines the roadmap for a national ICT-enabled transformation strategy.

CHAPTER 1

Why ICT-Enabled Transformation?

―

THE RISE OF THE NETWORKED SOCIETY

Smartphones, social networks, and mobile applications are all relatively recent phenomena. Yet they have already reshaped behaviors and lifestyles and brought individual and collective empowerment to large parts of the world. Access and connectivity have emerged as foundations for future progress. Megatrends such as urbanization, globalization, growing and aging populations, the rise of emerging markets, and climate change are affecting the way societies evolve and further stress the need to incorporate the full potential of ICT in social and economic development.

The performance of ICT continues to evolve exponentially as mobile and digital technologies expand into more and more areas of human existence. An abundance of data is generated from connections, sensors, and applications. The network is no longer a mere means of connection; it is an important source for data-driven innovation. New insights from data and information patterns provide opportunities to generate substantial value for business and society. Add to this development the radically reduced communication costs and the ease with which anyone today can access powerful tools and platforms and reach out to the markets, and we have some formidable ingredients for radical and disruptive innovation across industries, public services, and private life. In the years ahead, advances in and improved performance of ICT will offer people new ways to create, learn, produce, innovate, and influence our world in a positive way. We call this emerging society—of which we have seen only the beginning—the networked society.[1] In the networked society, most of the world's population will live in a culture of greater openness, sharing, collaboration, and self-organization, fundamentally changing the way we engage, innovate, and collaborate. A powerful ICT "interaction infrastructure," flat, shared, and largely invisible, will support the increasing flow of information. It will enable new experiences for a broad range of purposes and will serve as a foundation for innovation and transformation. Here are some distinctly new opportunities emerging from the adoption of ICT:

- **Power of us.** Culture, defined by collaboration and enabled by ICT, empowers individuals through social networking, recommendations, and peer reviews; shared real-time information in navigation; crowd sourcing as with Wikipedia; work opportunities for freelancers as with e-lance.com; and crowd funding where projects are funded from many contributions.
- **Instant society.** People demand information and service by companies through expanding channels 24-7. If their demand is not met, they find ways and means to share and distribute what they have, regardless of legal frameworks. For instance, a new episode of a TV serial must be available more or less at the same time globally (HBO, Netflix). In a global market, business is around the clock.
- **Digital values.** The music industry is a good example of how migration to digital platforms better serves the market, drives innovation, and builds consumer relationships and consumer engagement by creating a total experience. The financial sector

---

1 Manuel Castells first popularized the term "network society" in his book *The Rise of the Network Society* (1996). For more information on Ericsson's networked society vision please visit: http://www1.ericsson.com/thinkingahead/networked_society/.

on the other hand, has established new currencies and ultimately financial systems, such as bitcoin, loyalty points, likes, digital reputations, and identities.

* **Orchestration economy**. Business is using radically new collaboration models. Through its Connect and Develop initiative, Proctor & Gamble (P&G) generates 50 percent of all new products from collaborations with outside partners—that equates to more than four thousand products in the P&G portfolio. The Amazon e-business platform provides a ready-to-use, end-to-end solution for e-business. Airbnb connects property owners and travelers looking for cost-efficient alternatives to hotels.

* **Life as mosaic**. Networks are effectively blurring the boundaries between peoples, countries, and social identities that used to be clearly defined before. Liberated from the bonds of time and space, people inform, learn, give voice to their opinions, produce, market, and distribute ideas globally. Eventually, this will fundamentally change the way we work and the type of business operations and value-creating activities we engage in. It will change how businesses are organized, business development processes, work processes, as well as required skills and knowledge.

Technology changes economy and society at large. The era of automobiles and mass production, for example, has been one of mass markets, economies of scale, standardization, centralization, and hierarchies. In contrast, the guiding principles of the information age are decentralized integration, networks, adaptability, customization, knowledge as capital, innovation clusters, and economies of scope.

ICT-led transformation has, so far, been most evident in communication, media, finance, commerce, and some public sectors. Other sectors too will increasingly experience similar transformation, such as transportation, education and training, health care and wellness, energy, water, and sanitation. What used to be a well-defined shared model of innovation, production, distribution, and service offering, is being reshaped and redefined by new technology and the changing needs of society. At the same time there is ever-increasing pressure from megatrends such as urbanization, globalization, growing and aging populations, the rise of Asia, and climate change, resulting in the urgent need for greater efficiency in use of energy and natural resources.

Technological revolutions are accompanied by profound social and institutional changes. Hence, they encounter powerful resistance from established institutions, dominant vested interests, and incumbents. The new technoeconomic paradigm demands painful social and institutional changes, often disrupting, and even destroying, legacy systems, organizations, relationships, skills, routines, and work processes. Adoption of new technology is primarily a social process. It provides new opportunities for people, organizations, and society to essentially do the same things with less cost and effort or to do new things that were not previously possible. It also threatens incumbent interests by questioning existing modalities of value creation and established market positions. Realizing the transformational potential of the ICT revolution also requires redesigning or building new networks of institutions, transformation of regulatory frameworks and governance, new skills and competencies, and even radical changes to ideas and culture.

It is only when innovations are widely adopted by people, businesses, and public institutions that they can have a sustainable impact. Prevailing institutional and public policy frameworks can assist or constrain this impact. The role of the policy maker is of strategic importance in this milieu. It is to facilitate and lead the process of institutional and sociotechnical change, empower the change agents and innovators, and set the policy frameworks for the effective diffusion of new technologies. Sound public policy shapes and determines the duration, strength, distribution, and sustainability of the benefits of a networked society.

DEFINING TRANSFORMATION

As an integral part of the process of building a networked society and digital economy, transformation signifies deep structural changes in the economy and society brought about by the effective deployment and diffusion of ICT, and its by-product, the information revolution. The changes typically lead to increased use of information and communication resources and technologies; reduced cost and increased pace of transactions and interaction throughout the economy; full or partial digitization of information, products, services, and processes; empowerment of individuals, communities, and enterprises with connectivity and knowledge; and an increase in the share of information-based production and knowledge services in society. Transformation, therefore, is a radical improvement of societies' capabilities to get things done—to shape their physical, economic, social, and intellectual environments to their own ends.

Digital transformation is a shift to a new technoeconomic paradigm. ICT is a powerful and versatile transformative tool for all kinds of activities: financial services, education and health care, media and entertainment, public services, science and innovation, manufacturing, transportation and logistics, and more. Within organizations, this process goes beyond automation of existing activities to encompass redesigning and innovation of work processes and practices, and of the organizations that carry them out. It also involves dramatic increase in the generation and use of digitized data to analyze the social and natural environment, monitor resources, understand clients and partners, coordinate actions, deliver services, measure performance, improve policy making, and secure citizen feedback—almost in real time.

Effective adoption and use of ICT is measured only in part by e-readiness indicators, which do not tell the entire story, as they provide a static picture of inputs and outputs, and are not ends in themselves. The ends of transformation are, among others, to build sustainable and shared prosperity, eliminate poverty, provide effective and transparent governance, encourage a competitive and innovative economy, improve learning, and create a more open, mobile, and cohesive society. These outcomes will depend on the overall development vision, goals, public policy, and strategy of the country itself.

Thus, transformation is defined here in terms of

- **content**: structural transformation to a knowledge-based economy, fueled by the diffusion of ICT and the digitization of all types of transactions;
- **process**: transformation of the development process, enabling new modes of collaboration and partnership, new governance and business models, data-driven and transparent decision-making, smart management of resources and programs, open and networked innovation, broad participation, citizen empowerment, and grassroots-driven development;
- **pace**: transformation driven by fast-changing technology, dramatically improving communication, innovation, organizing, processing, coordinating, transacting, and sharing of knowledge and ideas;
- **ecosystem**: coherent transformation in policies and leadership institutions, ICT infrastructure, ICT industries and services, and digital applications in all sectors of the economy (Chapter 2).

Development is described as a process of social and economic transformation, of change and learning (Stiglitz, 1998; Rodrik, 2004, 2007). Digital transformation is about accelerating this transformation process with the power of new technologies. It promises to make development both sustainable and inclusive. It is about smart development, one that is relevant to both developed and developing countries alike.

A high-level panel of the United Nations (UN, 2013) stated on post-2015 global (sustainable) development goals that current approaches and pace of progress to date would not be sufficient to realize globally agreed development targets by 2030. It argued for a steep change in approach: "Business as usual thus cannot be an option and transformative change is needed." It argued for a "data revolution" and for capitalizing on the ongoing technology revolution to eradicate global poverty and secure shared prosperity (chapter 3). This reinforces the recognition of ICT as the crucial twenty-first-century tool for implementing development.

MAXIMIZING BENEFITS

A strategic approach to transformation would aim to maximize the benefits from ICT by taking into account interactions among key elements of the ICT ecosystem as they apply to each sector and across the entire economy. A significant degree of such interdependence has been realized in advanced knowledge economies. The Organisation for Economic Co-operation and Development (OECD) country studies provide evidence of significant "interaction effects," such as between investment in communication infrastructure, ICT applications, skill levels, and the policy environment (Economist Intelligence Unit, 2004). A critical mass of ICT development can have substantial positive impact on a country's economy. Chapter 2 proposes such a strategic and holistic approach to digital transformation.

For a developing country in particular, where information poverty is a vicious circle with multiple causes, the impact of one element of transformation is heavily dependent on progress in others. Investment in ICT requires investments in skills, process innovations, institutional changes, and policy reforms. Most successful countries have struck and maintained a balance between investments in the hard (ICT) and the soft (policy, human, and organizational) infrastructure. Studies of companies suggest the potential of ICT investments in improving productivity is highest when combined with changes in organizational processes and managerial practices.

There are many examples of interdependencies among key elements of the ICT ecosystem and of how they can be harnessed to maximize potential benefits. Content providers cannot operate without infrastructure suppliers. E-government cannot be inclusive and sustainable without a critical mass of users. Users require e-literacy, relevant content, affordable connectivity, and delivery channels to be developed at the same time. Programs that manage to orchestrate the various elements and bring together partners with diverse and complementary competencies can deliver significant and sustainable impact. Synergies create virtual cycles in which initial government and private investments attract other investors. For example, improving rural access via community information centers and Internet access centers attracts content developers and service providers, which in turn increases demand for infrastructure solutions and helps secure the financial viability of these centers.

A holistic strategy should optimize investments over time and across various elements of the ecosystem. Investment in the soft infrastructure is particularly relevant to the quality of implementation of transformation strategies. Singapore exemplifies such commitment to human resources and to optimizing investment across the ecosystem. Singapore also built technological foresight and technological scanning into their transformation strategies to fully utilize the advances offered by fast-changing ICT tools and platforms.

OVERCOMING BARRIERS AND MINIMIZING RISKS

The barriers to deep, sustainable changes in governments, institutions, power structures, practices, and behaviors must not be underestimated even as the ICT revolution moves forward.[2] Investments in ICT may be wasted and benefits not realized. Rising expectations of citizens for open and responsive government may be resisted by vested interests. ICT may become the control tool for the powerful rather than a tool

---

2 Most global ICT forums and national ICT policies have yet to adequately acknowledge and deal with the growing dark side of the ICT revolution and ethical aspects of the information society.

for empowerment, liberation, and inclusion. Below is a brief list of possible barriers and risks that should be addressed through national transformation efforts, and whenever possible, through global protocols and governance systems.

Vested interests and resistance to reforms. Transformation comes with winners and losers. Opening up markets for new entrants, securing completion in communication and ICT services, resisting monopolistic and protectionist behavior—all demand political leadership and social consensus on reforms. At the enterprise level, sharing information within and across institutions challenges entrenched habits of information hoarding and turf fending. Governments and political elites feel threatened by accountability and transparency and resist sharing data with civil society. Entrepreneurs adopt corrupt, unproductive, rent-seeking practices and thus block policy reforms. Understanding the barriers is essential to reform policies and regulations that will induce adoption of ICT and lead to transformation.

Wasting scarce development resources. Benefits from ICT investments are not automatic. They require complementary investments in human capital and much organizational and social learning. ICT-enabled restructuring is fraught with difficulties and risks even in industrial countries. The need for coherent and realistic policies to manage change and the integration of ICT into institutions cannot be overstated. ICT investments must also be subjected to cost-benefit analysis and placed in the context of other development priorities.

Unmet expectations. ICT facilitates new forms of information diffusion and social networks that empower civil society and individuals to challenge old forms of organization and governance, enabling new models of collective action and bottom-up development. These developments are a threat to authoritarian regimes, hierarchical structures, and industrial-age organizations. Transformation strategies should help governments and businesses retool their processes to meet citizen demands and feedback. Institutions unable or unwilling to rise to these challenges will become progressively unsustainable.

Eroding competitive positions. At the macrolevel, the fast-paced technological revolution is endangering the competitive positions of countries and their traditional industries and services, as it transforms them in dramatic ways. For some, the emerging global technoeconomic paradigm raises the bar for competing in the global marketplace; for others, it lowers entry barriers and multiplies the number of players in hypercompetitive markets.

Exacerbating inequalities. And what about the distribution of benefits? Will the ICT revolution herald the era of global economic inclusion or exacerbate inequalities and economic divides? The best defense of globalization and ICT diffusion is that hundreds of millions of people in developing countries are better off due to convergence (Spence, 2011). However, technological change always favors the prepared, and ICT has been the fastest technological change in history, thus exacerbating adjustment problems. It took a century for the printing press to reach fifty million people, forty years for the radio, four years for the Internet, and even less for mobile phones. Despite opportunities for leapfrogging, the lack of financial and human resources and other complementary factors, and the presence of "network externalities," suggest that many poor developing countries are likely to face the risk of a widening digital divide.[3] Within a country too, the digital divide may parallel similar disparities in income and access to other development services. Unless systematically addressed, this is a problem that is likely to grow.

The economics of information production and the global reach of the Internet can be a boon for consumers. But it can also thin out the professional workforce in many industries. Because ICT can perform symbolic processing, these technologies can augment or supplant humans in many information-processing tasks that historically were not amenable to mechanization. How will this influence the already skewed

---

3 Network externalities are derived from the fact that the value of a telephone line (and now the Internet) increases with each new subscriber by the number of potential connections between users (referred to as Metcalfe's law). This indicates substantial externalities, and there may be a threshold effect by which ICT begins to have real impact only at a certain penetration level in the economy.

income distribution in developing countries? Will outsourcing compensate for the concentration of wealth within developing countries or further exacerbate this trend? There is a natural desire to view the Internet as a leveling force that creates a fairer, more open, egalitarian, and democratic society, where economic opportunities are widely distributed. But experience in developed countries point to the replacement of both skilled and unskilled labor with software. The erosion of the middle class may accelerate as the divide widens between the digital elite and a large labor force whose incomes are disappearing.

It is important that these risks are managed as part of a holistic and inclusive digital transformation strategy. For the majority to benefit, it is assumed that compensatory actions will be initiated through redistribution of income, enhanced social protection, and investment in training and lifelong learning. These and other measures may lie beyond the control of technology policy makers and ICT planners, but they must be taken into account in formulating education and social policies for a networked society.

CHAPTER 2

The Strategy for Transformation

THE TRANSFORMATION ECOSYSTEM

The vast potential of ICT as a transformational enabler can be truly realized only through a holistic strategy. This guide advances a whole ecosystem view for ICT-enabled transformation, in order to pursue coherent policies and mutually reinforce ICT-enabled development initiatives at the national level (Figure 1). This framework helps identify

Figure 1: The Digital Transformation Ecosystem

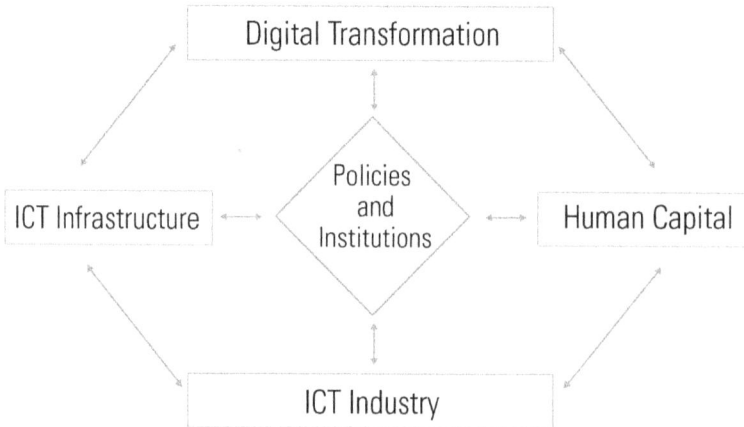

Source: Hanna, 2010, p. 246

key stakeholders to create an "ecosystem" for a networked society. It calls for shared visions and inclusive stakeholder mobilization. It maps the connections and relationships among diverse players concerned with supply and demand. It facilitates the creation of a national consensus on digital transformation and systematic thinking about ICT as the enabler of development. It also helps stakeholders identify weaknesses in the ecosystem that need to be addressed.

The digital transformation ecosystem can be conceived as composed of interdependent elements (Figure 1):

(a) ***Enabling policies and institutions.*** They constitute the environment that will either enhance or obstruct interaction among all other elements of the transformation process. They promote the effective supply and use of ICT in all sectors of economy and society. Enabling policies and institutions are essential to fostering trust in the digital economy. They are shaped by shared vision and leadership.

(b) ***Human capital.*** Skilled human resources are at the heart of the ICT revolution, both as users and producers; they include policy, technical, and change management skills as well as broad information and digital literacy, and technoentrepreneurship. The emphasis here is on transformational and user skills.

(c) ***ICT industry.*** A dynamic local ICT ecosystem is necessary to adapt global technology to local needs, manage and maintain technological infrastructure, develop digital local content and solutions, and effectively partner with global suppliers of ICT. In particular, local software development capability represents a core competency that enables wide and effective domestic use of new technologies.[4]

---

4 Some countries may have aspirations and capabilities to become global suppliers of technology, but that should not be done through protectionism and at the expense of fast adoption and local transformation of all other economic sectors (this topic is beyond the scope of this guide).

(d) ***ICT infrastructure.*** This refers to affordable and competitive communication infrastructure, including affordable access to the Internet, fixed and mobile narrow- and broadband, and other digital connectivity tools.

(e) ***ICT applications and institutional change.*** This component includes ICT applications and complementary investments in institutional capabilities to transform key sectors of the economy.

A holistic approach to transformation addresses the synergies and interdependencies in the evolving ICT ecosystem of a country. For example, the Internet and smartphones are mutually reinforcing. As of 2014, recent promising transformative technologies include mobile phones, smartphones,[5] fiber and wireless broadband, open data, big data and analytics, cloud computing, sensor networks, the Internet of Things, and 3-D printing. There are hundreds of thousands of mobile applications; their proliferation has been exponential since the introduction of the smartphone in 2007. Even the Internet, the most fundamental enabler of all ICT tools, continues to evolve.

The temptation with each new ICT tool is to treat it as the most transformative one, without regard to the rest of the building blocks, the whole ecosystem within which it must operate. Consider a recent set of cross-country econometric studies that predict the impact of broadband Internet (World Bank, 2012, among others), implying an automatic economic impact. However, overall current research suggests that broadband contributes to higher growth in countries with a critical mass of ICT adoption, reflecting return to scale. Broadband also has stronger productivity impact in sectors with high transactions, such as financial services. The impact of broadband on SMEs is likely to take a longer time to materialize, due to its slow accumulation of intangible capital and complementary capabilities. Conversely, broadband impact is higher when its adoption is combined with local incentives to innovate new applications.

---

5 By 2020, it is anticipated that most phones in the world will be smartphones.

Therefore, in the final analysis, the impact of broadband is neither automatic nor uniform across economies—it depends on its interactions with the rest of the ICT ecosystem and their evolution over time.

These findings reinforce the case for adopting holistic approaches to designing and planning for broadband use and nationwide ICT application, and for investing in the other transformation enablers mentioned earlier. A holistic approach will also involve building the pillars for using ICT to transform key sectors and common functions of an economy, while taking into account the many interdependencies among these pillars. Ignoring them can create crucial binding constraints to the whole digital transformation ecosystem.[6] Some of these interdependencies will emerge or become stronger during implementation and should be addressed in the context of an adaptive learning process.

PLANNING TRANSFORMATION

Three inputs are critical to the planning process: a) diagnosis of a countrywide ICT ecosystem (digital readiness assessment); b) identification of opportunities and threats present in the global environment; and c) in-depth review of the country's competitiveness or development strategy, and the role of information, communication, knowledge, and learning in realizing this strategy (Figure 2). These inputs will guide the creation of a shared vision of ICT-enabled transformation, identification of key stakeholders, and development and engagement of leadership institutions. From this, the broad directions for national digital policies and strategies will emerge. In turn, these strategic thrusts will help identify and prioritize transformation initiatives. The process may be carried out also at the sectoral and local levels, in continuous interaction with national-level activities, to ensure bottom-up initiative, broad ownership, and deep integration across sectors and levels. Striking the right balance between local and national initiatives is a constant challenge.

---

6 Draws on the theory of binding constraint in the management of organizations and in the diagnosis of economic growth.

Figure 2: The Digital Transformation Process

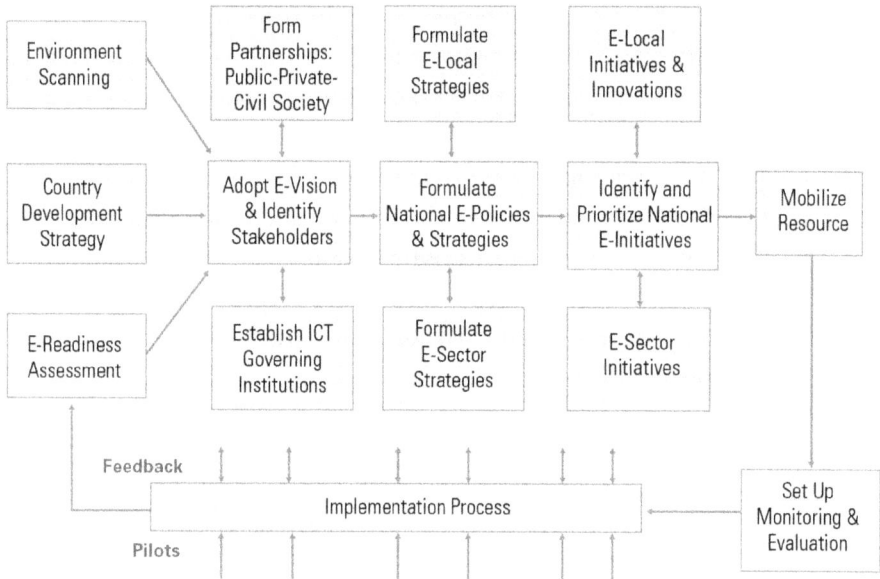

Source: Hanna, 2010a, page 19

The next step is to mobilize necessary resources from all partners and stakeholders. It may take many forms of public-private financing and innovative funding mechanisms to sustain the transformation process.

Holistic digital transformation faces varied implementation challenges. Countries have experienced significant vision-implementation (or aspiration-reality) gaps. These gaps need to be understood and systematically addressed. Goals and measurable indicators, monitoring and evaluation, and feedback channels must be established as early as possible during the planning process. Results of monitoring and evaluation will provide continuous assessment of progress, digital readiness, and development outcomes. As sustainable transformation takes time, often decades, measuring progress and demonstrating benefits are critical to political support for the process.[7] Integrating lessons from experience will speed up learning and reduce costs of ICT-enabled transformation.

TRANSFORMATION AS ADAPTIVE LEARNING

Successful countries perceive their digital transformation strategy not only as a policy document, but also as a dynamic and evolving process. A core challenge of digital transformation is to build capacity for agile learning, adaptive implementation, and transformative leadership. In this context, focusing on a blueprint—the strategy document—may hurt the country more than help it.

Integration of ICT into the economy and society is a complex sociotechnical process that requires experimentation, adaptation, social learning, and dexterous coordinating. An overall societal, political, and cultural change must take place, in which various kinds of technical, institutional, and social innovations interact with each other. This requires building momentum for effective deployment of ICT across the nation. The aim is to create dynamic comparative advantage by utilizing technological and institutional changes as driving forces of development, while harnessing intangibles such as knowledge and organizational and social capital.

Governments play several important roles as stakeholders: creating an enabling policy environment; dealing with institutional resistance, agency problems, and regulatory failures; correcting market and coordination failures; providing a platform for innovation and technological learning; and influencing change in other institutions through collective action. But governments cannot do it alone. In countries such as India, the private sector took the leading role. The Indian government

---

7   The time frame is a function of size of economy, local capabilities, leadership commitment, and sense of urgency. Singapore's move from a middle-income to a high-income economy, enabled by digital transformation, took about three decades.

has over time assumed strategic leadership as policy setter, a major user of ICT for the delivery of public services, investor in technical education, and coinvestor in the first generation of software technology and ICT services parks. Civil society participation was also essential to mobilize social entrepreneurship and social learning, and to overcome digital and development divides. Prospects for success substantially increase when governments work in close partnerships with business, civil society, and academia.

Transformation as "creative destruction" demands openness and innovation, and these in turn require a culture supportive of learning. Lessons of development suggest that it is a process of innovation, experimentation, learning, and ultimately, social and institutional transformation. Globalization and the ICT revolution have accelerated this process and opened up new options for development. Thus, creativity and learning take an even more important role than in the past in aiding the transformation process.

Strategic thinking is necessary not only at the planning stage, but also throughout implementation. Integrating ICT into development efforts requires using technology in new ways and in new contexts. Instruments and incentives used to promote ICT-enabled transformation work differently in countries with different levels of institutional maturity and technological capabilities. Governments, enterprises, and communities have to discover their own best practices or adapt promising international ones. They must engage in experimentation and pragmatic innovation for solutions that work in the local context. In economic literature, this is identified as a process of self-discovery (Rodrik, 2007). Business literature calls it an emergent strategy (Mintzberg et al, 1998).

At the country level the process of self-discovery involves identifying "first movers" and facilitating pockets of dynamism; scaling up and learning from the experience of pioneers to build a critical mass for reform and transformation; and finally, widening the process beyond existing clusters or islands of excellence into new innovation domains. At the enterprise or public-agency level, similar processes are at work: identifying promising innovation platforms; developing a portfolio of ICT-enabled transformation projects; scaling up successes into new services and practices; and finally, institutionalizing the process of enterprise-wide transformation. Leadership, vision, and national strategy play vital roles in enabling first movers, pilots, and bottom-up initiatives; scaling up successes and building critical mass; and institutionalizing the transformation process.

STRATEGIZING FOR NATIONAL TRANSFORMATION

A national strategy for digital transformation should therefore serve several pragmatic roles:

* Develop a shared vision, mobilize resources, and build coalitions for policy and institutional reforms.
* Devise policies and programs to overcome barriers to transformation.
* Clarify roles, build public-private partnerships, and facilitate participation by all stakeholders.
* Focus scarce resources on exploiting ICT for national priorities and help sequence and phase complementary investments.
* Promote digital inclusion, societal applications, bottom-up efforts, and scaling up of successful innovations.
* Leverage the potential of the ICT services industry in support of economy-wide competitiveness.
* Reorient national innovation to meet the learning requirements of ICT as the catalyst for productivity.
* Address failures, exploit network effects, secure investments, and accelerate learning.
* Monitor technological trends, anticipate implications for development and competitiveness. The faster and more disruptive the change, the more the need for foresight and adaptive capacity to integrate ICT in national transformation.

Part Two: Pursuing Transformation Possibilities

———

This second part, composed of three chapters, shows key steps in integrating digital transformation into national development and competitiveness strategies, benchmarking and assessing digital readiness, setting goals and targets, and mobilizing stakeholders. Frameworks and tools are suggested to help policy makers design transformation strategies for the whole government and for selected service sectors such as education and finance. The section covers ways to leverage mobile, open-government data, big data, and analytics to accelerate transformation.

CHAPTER 3

Integrating ICT-Enabled Transformation into Development

———

STAKEHOLDERS INVOLVED IN DIGITAL TRANSFORMATION should consider these issues:

- How should we go about developing a shared vision of national transformation?
- How can a national ICT strategy become integral to the national development and competitiveness strategy?
- How can ICT strategies be designed to attain global and national goals for inclusive and sustainable development?
- Why is a country diagnosis necessary, and what benchmarks and readiness indicators will help set goals and targets?
- What factors are to be considered in setting the scope and pace of change, and why are focusing, prioritizing, and sequencing important?

DEVELOP A SHARED VISION

Digital transformation strategy focuses on options and opportunities facilitated by ICT in the context of development and globalization. Corporate strategists and development planners have increasingly relied on agile processes and tools (Mintzberg, et al, 1998; Hanna and

Picciotto, 2002) for such a purpose. A creative, adaptive learning process is essential when dealing with fast-moving technologies in a dynamic global economy.

But where do we begin with our digital transformation strategy? Do we begin with the nation as a whole or with selected sectors? Should our strategy be based on ICT trends and their implications for the national economic strategy? Should we first focus on partial ICT interventions? Is there an optimal sequence to follow in order to maximize the benefits?

The scenarios in Figure 3 illustrate strategic thinking about the options by simplifying the range of potential country conditions and describing it along two distinct dimensions. Some countries have neither a comprehensive development strategy nor a holistic ICT strategy (scenario 1). Under this scenario, low payoffs and low sustainability are likely. An unclear development strategy and poor enabling environment can severely curtail the benefits of ICT (scenario 2). It is counterproductive and wasteful if national priorities remain unclear and substantial investment in ICT becomes an end in itself. Under such conditions, it is prudent to focus only on selective interventions in sectors where there are relatively clear development strategies, and complementary inputs exist for digital transformation.

A selective approach to leveraging ICT in the context of a clear and comprehensive development strategy may yield significant benefits, but it is limited to only those sectors where ICT is effectively deployed (scenario 3). Finally, evidence from leading countries suggests that the impact of ICT is highest when the development strategy is clear and ICT is utilized holistically for that development strategy (scenario 4). To move to this last scenario that will maximize the development impact of their ICT investments and create a sustainable ICT-enabled transformation ecosystem, countries must think holistically and simultaneously about ICT and development strategies, plan and experiment to integrate both strategies in a dynamic way, and open up new options for development.

Figure 3: Strategies for Integrating ICT and Development

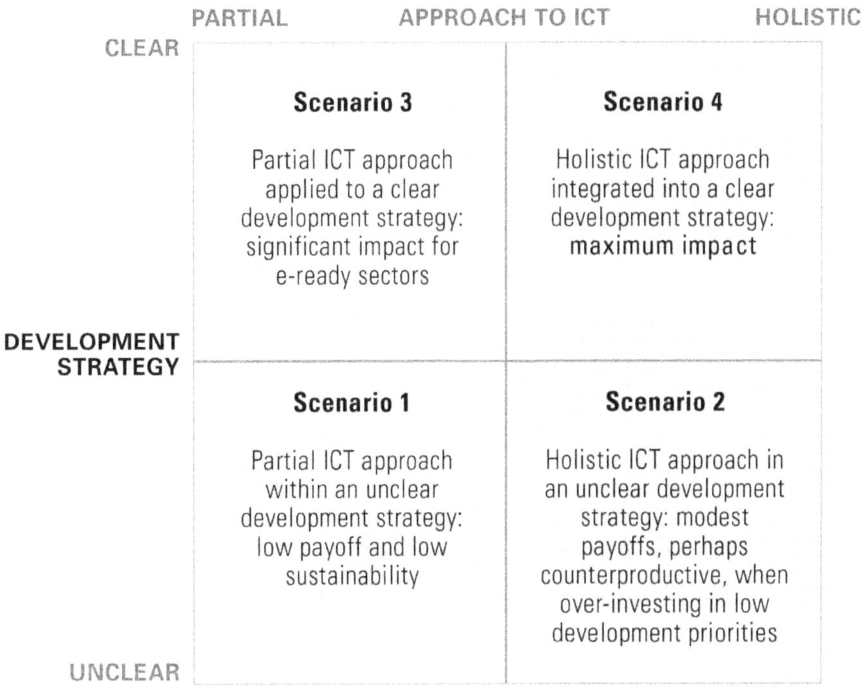

PARTIAL   APPROACH TO ICT   HOLISTIC

CLEAR

Scenario 3	**Scenario 4**
Partial ICT approach applied to a clear development strategy: significant impact for e-ready sectors	Holistic ICT approach integrated into a clear development strategy: **maximum impact**

DEVELOPMENT
STRATEGY

Scenario 1	**Scenario 2**
Partial ICT approach within an unclear development strategy: low payoff and low sustainability	Holistic ICT approach in an unclear development strategy: modest payoffs, perhaps counterproductive, when over-investing in low development priorities

UNCLEAR

Source: Hanna, 2010a, page 21

Interactions between strategies for ICT for economic development are not a one-time event. They help shape and are shaped by a shared vision and the role of ICT in the transformation process. They evolve over time, in response to mutual adjustments, experimentation, learning, and discovery. They are not the product of a single leader or institution, but are nurtured by many institutions and champions of transformation. They are based on continuous dialogue among government reformers and business leaders on the one hand, and ICT suppliers and strategists on the other. Therefore, such interactions should be integrated in the digital leadership institutions and policy-making mechanisms of a country.

A vision of transformational change leading to the networked society should present a compelling narrative about the future for all stakeholders. It should also provide guidance for the prioritization of transformation projects and programs best tailored for a given country. However, some general guidelines may be useful.

- *Start with the end in mind.* What does "transformative development" mean? Why do we aspire for a networked society? What will it be like to live in an inclusive information society? What does transformation mean for youth, women, rural, and marginalized groups? Leaders must present in concrete terms to diverse stakeholders how the vision will be realized. They must answer the question: What will this change mean for *me*?
- *Clearly articulate priorities across sectors.* A vision emphasizing an empowered and productive rural population, for example, would imply giving priority to rural access and connectivity, content, multipurpose rural information centers, information literacy, rural entrepreneurship, applications that serve the local government, and local service delivery. The vision would also draw attention to synergies and complementarities among these elements of transformation in the rural areas. Alternatively, for an advanced urban society, such a vision may give priority to sustainability, resilience, smart cities, smart growth, innovation clusters, and other aspects of a knowledge economy enabled by ICT.
- *Prioritize a shared infrastructure.* A national vision of digital transformation should place high priority on a shared (common and reusable), scalable, and dynamic (open, flexible) information infrastructure; human resources capability development; and effective methods to solve cross-sectoral interdependencies. It should be the basis for prioritizing, sequencing, and phasing, thus accommodating initial constraints, while exploring potential synergies.

- *Promote collaboration among key players.* Partnering among major players helps to attract private investment, while encouraging network opportunities in public and private sectors, the education system, civil society, and with other stakeholders. For example, when governments create favorable conditions for collaboration among ICT businesses and the education system, the private sector may upgrade the education system to meet the demand of business with qualified ICT professionals.

- *Seek synergies in competing stakeholder visions.* A dynamic national vision must build consultative and learning mechanisms to adapt to major changes in the national and global political environment. In the first digital transformation program in Sri Lanka in 2002, there were several narrow and competing visions of what ICT may contribute to the development of the country. A deliberate effort was initiated to engage various stakeholders in creating a shared vision by drawing upon the synergies among them. A process such as this may evolve over time to reflect changes in the local and global contexts.

- *Link the national vision to local initiatives.* Grassroots initiatives are often led by NGOs with donor support. They attempt to deliver quick results, create local champions, and provide valuable lessons. However, relying exclusively on "low-hanging fruit"—easily implementable pilots—can fragment resources and diminish national capacity to deliver long-term, cross-sectoral, and strategic solutions. Priority should be given to replicable, scalable, and sustainable pilots that also share the national vision and help to advance national goals for transformation.

PURSUE GLOBAL DEVELOPMENT GOALS

As part of developing a compelling narrative and clear destination, policy makers may consider linking their digital transformation strategy to the post-2015 development goals articulated by the United Nations

(2013). Where does ICT fit in with the global development agenda? Where does ICT fit in with a country's development agenda, without straying from the global consensus on development goals?

Researchers and practitioners in ICT for development tend to live in a "bubble" [8] (Heeks, 2014). Among aid agencies, ICT is isolated, dominated by technologists, and not adequately connected to global development goals. In most developing countries, the national ICT agenda is led by the ministries of ICT or by telecom regulatory agencies. ICT policies and strategies are often pursued independent of the country's development strategies and rarely viewed as enablers of transformation. Current tools for assessment of country readiness reinforce the exclusive concern with the technical components of readiness and availability (access), while neglecting adoption, use, and impact. These practices must change for policy makers and aid agencies to realize transformative development.

One promising way is to explicitly link national ICT strategies to global and national development objectives.[9] To address environmental goals, policy makers may stress the use of ICT to monitor and improve the environment, and mitigate and adapt to climate change. They may link ICT to attaining resilient and sustainable global and sectoral development goals. For example, how will ICT policies and strategies address poverty eradication? How can ICT mobilize finance for development and make finance more inclusive? How will ICT be diffused and made effective to generate jobs and make other sectors of the economy more productive and competitive? Should ICT be used to fight corruption and make public services work for the poor? Should ICT be used to improve urban planning, governance, and services? How can we ensure that ICT can be a tool for inclusive development?

---

8   This is also the case in policy debates on ICT among the most advanced countries. The debates are usually led by technologists or specialized ICT agencies, with little participation from other disciplines or stakeholders.

9   Heeks (2014) argues for making similar explicit links to set the new priorities for ICT4D research in a post-2015 world.

To answer these questions digital transformation leaders must speak the language of development with other stakeholders. Even so, specific answers for a country may not emerge fully at the outset. They may have to be invented, reimagined, and experimented with during the course of transformation.

BENCHMARK AND ANALYZE SWOT

A holistic country diagnosis can provide a solid start for setting strategic priorities and realistic targets.

Tools, methodologies, and indicators for assessing and ranking country readiness for the networked world have mushroomed. As with any other tool, benchmarking can be misused and should be clearly understood and used with care. These indices and their underlying methodologies have their limitations—for example, keeping out dimensions difficult to measure. They should be properly interpreted in relation to specific national circumstances and only then used as an input to a Strength-Weakness-Opportunity-Threat (SWOT) analysis, target setting, and strategy development.

Broadly stated, digital readiness assessments measure a country's ability to exploit ICT for human, economic, or democratic development. They help identify underlying issues of technical and human capacity that will need to be addressed to effectively implement ICT for transformation. However, readiness assessments cannot substitute for—but can help to engage stakeholders directly in—a national dialogue on goals, targets, and priorities for digital transformation.

Both vision and strategy should be guided by in-depth information about a country's digital readiness and positioning in the global economy. Several methodologies have been developed and used by organizations to establish rankings for telecommunication infrastructure, human capital, online services, global competitiveness, innovation, etc. The World Economic Forum developed the Networked Readiness Index (NRI); the United Nations developed the e-Government

Development Index (EGDI); and the World Bank has the Knowledge Economy Index (KEI).

The International Telecommunication Union (ITU) continues to publish its series on *Measuring the Information Society*. It features two benchmarking tools: the ICT Development Index (IDI) and the ICT Price Basket (IPB). The former captures progress in ICT development in 155 countries through a composite index of eleven indicators. The latter tracks the cost and affordability of ICT in more than 160 countries through a composite index of fixed-line, mobile, and broadband tariffs over time. Efforts continue to be made to develop partnerships on measuring ICT for development, including one led by ITU and the UN Conference on Trade and Development (UNCTAD). Many other indices have emerged to cover different aspects of digital readiness and benchmarking.

The Networked Readiness Index (NRI) of the World Economic Forum is a good example of a holistic approach to measure access to and impact of ICT (Box 1).

Box 1: The Networked Readiness Index (NRI)

The NRI aims at measuring the capacity of economies to fully leverage ICT for increased competitiveness and development, building on a mixture of hard data collected by international organizations such as the ITU, the World Bank, and the United Nations, and survey data from the Executive Opinion Survey, conducted annually by the World Economic Forum in each of the economies covered – 144 developed and developing economies (2014).

The Networked Readiness Framework underlying the NRI assesses:
- the presence of an ICT-friendly **environment**, by looking at a number of features in the country's business sector, some regulatory aspects, and soft and hard infrastructure for ICT;
- the level of ICT **readiness** of the three main national stakeholders – individuals, the business sector, and the government; and
- the actual **use** of ICT by the above three stakeholders.

ICT impact sub-index, a fourth sub-index, has been added since 2012, to measure the effect of ICT on both the economy and society, a complex but increasingly important task.

Over a decade, the NRI has evolved and grown in scope. The index now includes the creation of new skills crucial to an information-rich society, access to digital resources, software and skills, and proxies of social and economic impact. Thus, it aims to identify areas where investment, regulation, and incentives can accelerate the impact of ICT.

UN's EGDI measures digital development in governments across 193 UN member states. It is a composite index based on the weighted average of three normalized indices: a government online services index, a telecommunications infrastructure index, and a human capital index. The online services indicator particularly has been evolving to get a better understanding of the transformation process. While the EGDI focuses on various factors affecting the delivery of a successful digital transformation program, ITU's IDI index centers on broader ICT indicators, and both NRI and the World Bank's KEI work on a much broader evaluation of economic and social factors impcting the use of ICT.

The short-lived Office of the e-Envoy in the United Kingdom compared the progress of digital strategy in the country and gathered and analyzed best practices from around the world, with emphasis on e-Government. The European Union has also been benchmarking digital public services in Europe across twenty basic services. These tools and indicators provide insight into initial conditions in a country, help with global analyses, and benchmarking countries against comparators and competitors. However, assessments also represent heavy investments in data collection, with primary attention given to international rankings. Instead they should be aimed at mobilizing local stakeholders, and helping local actors design and implement their national ICT strategies.

The world of measurement is evolving to meet new expectations. The World Economic Forum has recently refined its framework to increase focus on the measurement of outcomes. The European Commission benchmarking survey is placing greater emphasis on piloting and broadening its coverage of the local level. The UN and other aid agencies are placing greater emphasis on outcomes and the impact of ICT on development. New ICT indicators are planned for the post-2015 Millennium Development Goals (MDG).

Despite their limitations, digital readiness assessments function as pointers to broad areas requiring improvement. They provide a useful start for a national dialogue among stakeholders, attract attention of policy makers, and help build coalitions for reform. All the same, assessments ultimately provide static analysis and cannot substitute for a strategic approach. A strategic framework balances priorities within resource constraints; allows for a dynamic learning process; helps engage stakeholders in downstream strategy formulation and implementation; and establishes systems for monitoring progress and evaluating results to streamline managing transformation.

A SWOT analysis draws on information gathered from country rankings and assessments, from indicators that contribute to composite indices, and from qualitative inputs by key stakeholders. It also benefits from a deeper understanding of technological trends such as open data, big data and analytics, wireless broadband, cloud computing, and the associated opportunities and risks. A SWOT analysis does not produce a specific transformation strategy, but it can help generate strategic options that, in turn, can guide and enrich the search for common strategic thrusts, goals, and targets.

SET THE PLANNING HORIZON

Goals and targets must be based on local considerations—aspirations, funding resources, political dynamics, and capability to absorb technological change. Countries often take a short-term perspective, driven by political considerations, and limited appreciation of the requirements of initiating and sustaining change. Some elements of digital transformation demand long-term planning, while others need short-term targets. Communication infrastructure, and institutional and human resources development for a networked society are best addressed within a term of seven to ten years. Some of the building blocks for transforming government or public sector take time to develop, although cloud computing and mobile-based delivery of services are enabling faster adaptation.

On the other hand, developing policies, ecosystems for mobile apps and open data, applications for government and society, can be pursued with short- and medium-term goals, and benefit from experiences of frontrunner countries.

Choices of specific goals and targets should be informed by past progress, current situational analysis supported by surveys of users and suppliers, and benchmarks and rankings of comparator countries in areas such as networked readiness. One recommended approach for follower countries is to have their targets informed by progress of countries ahead of them in their transformation journey but close to their overall socio-economic development. Goals and targets may be refined over time based on frequent surveys and feedbacks from stakeholders, and agile monitoring and evaluation systems.

Transformation strategies should focus efforts, resources, and leadership attention on producing tangible results, creating momentum and political support, matching the availability of local resources and capabilities, and ensuring sustainability. Many countries have vision statements that are "all encompassing in scope without being strategic or actionable" (UNDP ICT Taskforce Series 3, 2003). Without a strategic focus, the planning process could be hijacked by special interests, or spread too thinly on many initiatives, thus fragmenting into unfinished projects.

Transforming Government

———

To be effective, ICT adoption in the public sector must combine with complementary investments in human capacity, institutional practices, and policy reform. Policy makers should therefore be clear about their national objectives for transforming government, and seek answers to the following questions:

- Why should we transform government?
- What makes a whole-of-government approach necessary and cost-effective?
- Why should we adopt shared infrastructures?
- Why is demand mobilization critical to sustainable changes in public services, and what are the best practices?
- Why should mobile government be a priority and what can it offer?
- What can big data and analytics tools offer as part of transforming government and what are the best practices?
- What is the promise of open government data and how can it be realized?

IMPERATIVES FOR TRANSFORMING GOVERNMENT

Governments all over the world face a potent combination of challenges today: increasing budget shortfalls; rising public expectations for services; growing inequalities in incomes and opportunities; declining trust in government for failing to deliver on promises; and the need to compete in a fast-moving, knowledge-based global economy.

Although literature on the subject of digital government mostly focuses on technology, isolated applications, and incremental change, government transformation must be envisaged in the context of reform and development. The imperatives for such transformations in developing nations are further driven by severe financial constraints, poor infrastructure and public services, unmet basic needs, fragile democracies, weak governance, high levels of inequalities, and widespread information poverty. As transformational changes are inherently more risky and benefits take time to realize typically beyond electoral cycles, there is often a bias toward incremental change.

Most governments face budget pressures and shortfalls, caused by increased demand for services combined with insufficient tax revenues. In higher and middle-income countries, aging populations add a huge burden to health, pension, and other support systems. In developing countries, budget pressures are more acute and are caused by additional factors such as fast growing populations, nascent social protection systems to compensate for economic volatility, global competition for foreign direct investment (FDI) through tax reductions, and drying up of traditional sources of revenue such as tariffs on trade. New public initiatives are often introduced when the economic outlook is promising. Subsequently, when cyclical budget shortfalls occur, politicians faced with a backlog of unmet popular demands are reluctant to cut the programs.

Citizens and businesses today expect demonstrable results and better responsiveness from governments. This is particularly the case with middle-income developing countries where multinationals are setting the standards through their global services, client support, and their own service requirements from local governments. Citizens expect to be connected to government information, services, and assistance anytime, anywhere.

There are also the challenges of rising income inequality and asymmetric access to information, knowledge and opportunities. In many poor countries, public services are exclusively available to the wealthy and the urban middle class, if at all. Whatever public services are offered, they are of poor quality, provided inefficiently at high costs, and are a major source for bribery and corruption (World Bank, 2004). As new technologies are implemented, governments face the further challenge of making public services accessible to all citizens through multiple channels. A digital divide further reinforces the service divide by reducing pressure from well-served classes to improve public services across the board.

Governments all over, but especially among the poorer developing countries, encounter declining trust and legitimacy when they fail to deliver basic services and security to large segments of their populations. Democracies are particularly vulnerable as social and political forces press for decentralization, while economic forces demand integration with regional and global economies. This crisis of political institutions and democratic governance can be construed as a unique opportunity to review how new technologies can assist in a holistic reform of the public sector (Rubino-Hallman and Hanna, 2006).

The speed with which capital flows around the world in search of higher returns demands more innovative governance. Globally integrated and demand-responsive supply chains are setting standards for customs, ports, logistics, and trade facilitation. Governments are pressed to modernize infrastructures and processes. The "cost of doing business" is open for all to examine, and countries are benchmarked annually in the globally competitive race to attract investment (IFC, 2013). Not surprisingly, businesses are often strong allies and advocates of digital governance in an effort to simplify operations. Growth and economic development are in significant part determined by how the government can intelligently regulate and facilitate business participation in the global economy.

Success in knowledge societies increasingly depends on communication, information, and innovation. The more rapid the pace of change, more novel the challenge, greater is the need for knowledge-based learning and adaptive organizations. Non–routine problems allow little time to react, and involve a high cost of failure. When governments manage programs requiring complex administrative technologies and partnerships across the board, responsibility for solving problems is diffused among organizations locally and globally. This is where innovative solutions are required that draw upon instant information and communication, situation-based coordination, network-based approaches, and boundary-spanning performance management (Kettl and Kelman, 2007).

All these imperatives suggest moving beyond ad hoc adjustments to sustained transformational change in public sector management. They dramatically increase the stakes associated with the pace of government reform. They demand painful integration of entrenched silos, partnerships with business and civil society, and enabling employees to be part of the change through retooling and reskilling.

OBJECTIVES AND USES OF E-GOVERNMENT

Reform objectives and visions should help define the broad directions of public sector transformation and the use of ICT to enable this transformation. By deriving investment priorities in ICT from reform objectives, policy makers can avoid supply-driven solutions and secure alignment of ICT investments with reform objectives.

There is a vast and growing literature on e-government applications (Hanna, 2010a). Common e-government applications may be classified in terms of enabling public sector reforms in five areas: efficiency and resource management; access and quality of public services; investment climate and private sector competitiveness; transparency, accountability, and participation in governance; and policy making and knowledge management. Each area covers multiple objectives and corresponding applications. To prioritize and sequence the applications, policy makers should be aware of proven ICT applications and be clear about the reform objectives being pursued.

Improving efficiency and resource management requires ICT applications that:

* increase public sector productivity;
* promote outsourcing and partnerships with private sector and civil society;
* improve public resource mobilization and expenditure management;
* enhance civil service management;
* increase competitiveness and lower transaction costs of public procurement; and
* simplify and reengineer government processes.

Improving public services requires applications that:

* improve quality and reach of basic public services such as taxes, licenses, permits, certificates, and land titles;
* support health, education, and lifelong learning;
* provide choice and competition in service delivery via information brokerage and public-private partnerships; and
* reduce transaction costs to citizens via one-stop service centers, citizen-centric portals, among others.

Global competition is driving governments to improve their business climate and provide effective support services to their SMEs. Public sector reforms to reduce transaction costs to business, to support entrepreneurship and SME development, and to facilitate trade are significantly enabled by e-government applications. The use of ICT can streamline administrative procedures and reduce transaction costs between business and government. Electronic public procurement, for example, is an area where results can be demonstrated early and clearly in terms of efficiency, agility and transparency. Similarly, ICT can provide business support services to SMEs and facilitate their access to finance. ICT applications can also support investment promotion by providing investors access to information on polices and regulations.

ICT applications can also help to reform governance by enabling citizen feedback, making public procurement open and transparent and by facilitating information sharing on budgets and financial performance. Electronic performance indicators and performance management systems can track decisions and outcomes and engage citizens in policy development. By promoting transparency, ICT applications can enable effective decentralization. They can also help enforce the rule of law and modernize the legislature and judiciary.

Finally, policy making and knowledge management too stand to gain significantly from the emergence of big data, analytics, and open data and rapidly growing mobile apps.

ADOPT A WHOLE-OF-GOVERNMENT ARCHITECTURE AND INFRASTRUCTURE

A whole-of-government (WOG) approach uses enterprise-wide architecture (EA) and Government Interoperability Framework (GIF) to transform core government processes, and secure interoperability, connectedness, and information sharing across departments. This requires the adoption of common standards for all agencies to integrate their data, business processes, and service delivery applications and channels. However, there is no one-size-fits-all solution for WOG to succeed. Singapore, for example, focused its WOG effort on an enterprise architecture program as the foundation for future initiatives.[10] The WOG approach is increasingly part of ICT strategies around the world. It has been a focus area in Singapore's strategic plan (Hanna and Knight,

---

10   http://www.egov.gov.sg/egov-programmes/programmes-by-government/whole-of-government-enterprise-architecture-wog-ea

2012). The United States and the United Kingdom have adopted different models, more selective and centralized.

One important tool to realize economies of scale and customer-centered government is to organize common business processes across agencies and around user needs. These may involve front-office business processes, such as a shared call center, and a common portal for online contact with enterprises. They may also cover shared back-office business processes, such as procurement, financial management, and human resources management (Figure 4).

Figure 4: E-Government Architecture

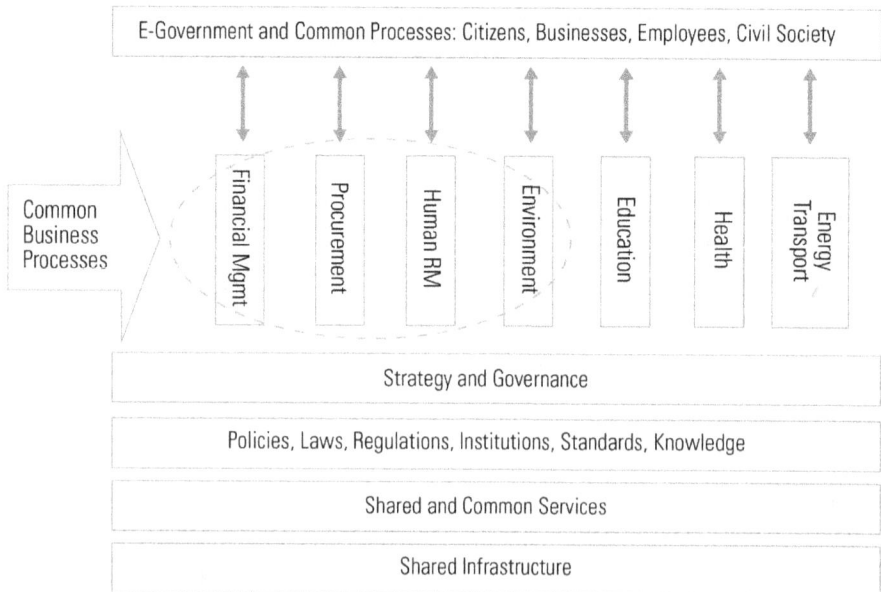

Source: Hanna, 2010b, p. 132

Shared processes across government agencies help overcome silos of public administration. The benefits can be substantial for developing countries where duplication and fragmentation abound. Common business processes across agencies reduce wasteful duplication. By reexamining and standardizing common processes, a single solution can be diffused and reused many times over. This approach also expedites information sharing across agencies and reduces user burden of reporting. It allows agencies to focus on core activities by providing them with the option of outsourcing standardized processes. Such outsourcing, increasingly enabled by cloud computing, helps create economies of scale and centers of excellence. Consolidating ICT expertise in support of common business processes too can capture economies of scale. Making elements of service delivery common raises awareness of overlaps and inconsistencies across programs and creates pressures for alignment and administrative simplification (OECD, 2005).

Countries vary in levels of cooperation among agencies. Some agencies may limit cooperation to information sharing, and set up a knowledge center to facilitate knowledge exchange on common business processes, or agree on a referential model of standardized processes. Other more cooperative agencies may decide to share some databases and IT systems, and create a shared service center. At the highest level of coordination, the shared service center becomes a separate organization. Approaches to adoption of common business processes vary from top-down control, mandating the use of a common solution, to a facilitating approach, using incentives, to a *laissez-faire* passive role for the central government. Country factors—ranging from culture, legislation, and politics, to public administration traditions—influence these choices.

In Korea, the special committee for e-government analyzes all processes and develops mandatory common solutions at the federal and municipal levels. In Germany, the e-government agency is not empowered to impose mandatory use of common processes. In the United States, the e-government office in the Office of Management and Budget (OMB) uses federal and agency EA to identify common processes and then uses the budget process to align all major IT investments with this common view for shared solutions.

Implementing common business processes raises many challenges. Involved agencies must be convinced of the benefits. Clear communication of advantages and results is critical. It is easier to start small, perhaps in one agency, to show early results, and scale up. Potential users may participate early on in the development and implementation of such processes, through advisory boards or steering committees representing involved agencies. It is also important to agree on mechanisms to share costs and revenues. Expectations too must be managed, recognizing upfront costs, and the lag in realizing benefits. Clear implementation responsibilities should be set at the highest levels. It is essential to promote cultural change to make collaboration the norm.

Similar principles and challenges apply to sharing communication infrastructures (government-wide networks), resources (such as skilled ICT and security staff), facilities (such as payment systems, delivery channels), and services. Policy makers should regularly explore ways to encourage such sharing, so as to economize on scarce resources, and maximize flexibility and information sharing.

MOBILIZE DEMAND AND MONITOR ADOPTION OF E-SERVICES

Unlocking the potential of e-government depends on high-levels of uptake of e-services. The United Kingdom, for example, promotes a clearly branded, single, citizen-centric, all-of-government site. User segmentation by audience and topic ensures consistent navigation. High-value services are targeted based on analysis of user needs. The one-stop business link website has been developed through cross-agency collaboration in response to feedback from small businesses and changes in business environment. In Germany, the government has set up user councils to support agencies of central and regional government.

Mobilizing demand and educating users are greater challenges in developing countries where there is little awareness among the masses and low ICT literacy. Marketing of people-friendly websites, development of a single e-government brand, and a consistent navigation with a common look and feel are a best practice, as in Canada and Australia. High uptake is also a consequence of high value services requiring collaboration across agencies. Affordable connectivity is also critical to building a wide user base.

Government transformation programs should be tailored to take account of the country's ability to adopt and integrate ICT applications in public agencies. These programs may benefit from e-readiness exercises already conducted for the economy as a whole (chapter 3), or go beyond the metrics of general e-readiness assessments and consider factors specific to the applications they are considering. As with country e-readiness, government e-readiness and benchmarking should not be viewed as an end in itself, but only as a process to engage stakeholders and form coalitions for reform.

In assessing the needs and capabilities of citizens to utilize e-government services, planners should take into account the fact that a large percentage—possibly a vast majority—of citizen interactions with government services will continue to be in person or over the telephone. In Ireland, for example, the Information Society Commission indicated that in developing e-government services, the readiness of citizen groups to use self-service channels must be considered, as must the complexity and requirements of the service. A high proportion of interactions are in the areas of health and social services where citizens tend to be elderly, in poor health, and from lower education and income brackets, many of whom may not benefit from a self-service channel.

To benchmark and monitor, the supply and demand of online services can be viewed from separate perspectives. Demand-side metrics are designed to track use of, and satisfaction with, e-government. They can include measurements of user attitudes and preferences for services, as well as barriers to usage. Demand-side indicators require user surveys. Supply-side metrics measure the availability and sophistication of online services. They can include portal or e-service benchmarks such as availability of portals and applications, or sophistication of functionality;

and management performance benchmarks such as measurements of government progress toward stated goals, including agency-by-agency status. Most indicators can be captured through Internet surveys.

It is important to be clear about the purpose and audience of e-government benchmarking. It can inform policy makers of progress and past achievements. It can assist them in setting prospective directions for high e-government performance. An often neglected but important purpose is accountability. Often neglected audiences for benchmarking are citizens and civil society organizations.

The nature of benchmarking is likely to change in line with the maturity of the program and corresponding change in e-government policy issues (Heeks, 2009). While advanced countries may have moved beyond issues of e-readiness and availability to focus on service uptake and impact, for a majority of the world's nations many elements of readiness for e-government appear to be part of the policy agenda, and rightly so. Most e-government programs in developing countries still face challenges in terms of legal, institutional, human, leadership, and technological infrastructure; and standards for services are moving targets.

In defining Key Performance Indicators (KPI), countries use a range of metrics including: number of agencies and functions online, download rates for forms and reports, usage rates for various services, reduction in average processing time for requests and applications, reduction in number of complaints, increased citizen participation in consultations, lower costs to government in service delivery, lower costs to citizens and businesses in utilizing services, and user satisfaction. Since what gets measured gets done, using benchmarks and indicators not relevant to specific country contexts can be wasteful and misleading.

The European Commission (EC) has developed a common benchmark measurement, the i2010, which has been applied annually since 2001 to measure progress on e-government (EC, 2009). The benchmarking now covers 27 member countries, using indicators for supply and demand perspectives that are critical to e-government implementation. It focuses on "20 basic services" offered through 14,000 public-service provider websites across Europe. The measurement has generated trends and patterns that describe the progress of leapfroggers, fast growers, moderate adopters, and those leading countries whose e-service supply (availability and sophistication) has reached saturation. The system has proven to be a valuable policy-informing tool.

One key insight from the EC benchmarking is that the gap between putting services online and the service being used tends to persist beyond the anticipated time lag. In some countries Internet use and broadband penetration are low. Other reasons are lack of awareness and lack of added value. This calls for a better understanding of how to attract, engage, and incentivize citizens. The EC benchmarking system is continuing to evolve, to reflect the maturity of e-government programs among the leading member countries, and to add new services of current relevance such as energy and environment. The evolving system enables dynamic and long-term policy discourse.

The economic crisis of 2008 that led to high levels of public debt emphasized the need for measuring the efficiency of government and continuous upgrading of e-government benchmarking. It drew attention to government-wide productivity improvements through better analytics, smart regulation, reduced administrative burdens on business, increased sharing of information, and cross-agency collaboration. Better visibility of expenditure by government, and more efficient transactions between government and suppliers (through e-procurement) are promising targets for considerable savings.

In developing countries, e-government surveys, report cards, and global benchmarking exercises have been focused on the supply side, such as the features and functionalities of websites, rather than the fundamental nature of ICT-enabled transformation and the factors supporting demand and change. Such surveys need to include metrics on networking and collaboration as well as the role of e-government in inducing innovation.

Demand-side metrics may be developed as part of the stakeholder consultation process. Increasing the "voice of the user" in e-government planning can also help identify KPIs or other metrics for monitoring implementation. Stakeholder consultation at all stages may prevent investments too far ahead of user interest and capacity. This consultation process is particularly critical in developing countries where the voice of the user is often weak or poorly understood, and where central planners are often distant from the realties on the ground. Focus on the end user may also help change the mindset of public sector employees from a traditional agency-centric thinking into a customer-centric one.

One reason for the slow uptake of online services is the digital divide. Even in the United States, broadband Internet adoption, as well as computer use, varies across demographic and geographic groups. Lower income families, people with less education or with disabilities, blacks, Hispanics, and rural residents generally lag behind. Other explanations include a mismatch between e-services and citizen demand; lack of awareness or IT skills; and lack of competition and affordability of ICT services.

Few governments promote their services offline or help users online: in 2012, only about 47 countries provided information on how citizens use services on their websites, a proxy indicator for the governments' interest in usage. Yet citizens generally embrace online services when they are made aware of them (Australian Government Information Management Office, 2011).[11] The Australian government portal now offers navigation by services, people, topics, and life events, enabling a choice in finding the appropriate task in an intuitive manner.[12]

---

11 http://www.finance.gov.au/publications/interacting-with-government-2011/index.html

12 http://australia.gov.au/services
http://australia.gov.au/people
http://australia.gov.au/topics
http://australia.gov.au/life-events

Stimulating usage is also a design issue. Sweden's government page has long excelled in allowing users to tailor website settings and providing a simplified language version, a video of sign language, and having the website read its text out loud, among other features.[13]

LEVERAGE MOBILE

The mobile phone has emerged as a ubiquitous distribution and delivery platform for online services. With fast growing penetration of mobile phones even among the poorest and the most remote areas of the globe, mobile online services (m-government) are the new frontier in the delivery of public services.

M-government acts as an additional channel for speedy interaction with all stakeholders, including policy makers, service providers, consumers, and other representatives of society. Mobile tools provide public service personnel the convenience of entering data and information even while they are out of the office and on the field. They extend the reach of online services beyond common information centers of government, to the underserved constituents. Most importantly, they can be used to innovate new services and transform governance. This last stage requires deep changes to government processes and response capacity.

Some countries are moving to leverage this new channel for public service delivery. In Singapore, citizens enjoy a variety of services available through wireless technologies, with text messaging the most popular way of sharing information between the government and its citizens. The government uses SMS (Short Messaging Service) alerts for a variety of services, such as renewal of road tax, medical examinations for domestic workers, passport renewal notifications, parking reminders, and parliament notices and alerts. Singapore government has since deployed over 300 m-services and its plan for 2011–2015 is to create more

---

13 Change of setting: http://regeringen.se/sb/d/6910
Sign language video: http://regeringen.se/sb/d/8962
Simplified language version: http://regeringen.se/sb/d/2506

innovative m-services. However, most governments are at early stages of mobile-induced transformation.

Many advanced countries have identified mobile technologies as key to government transformation strategy. Countries where smartphones are common, governments have begun to create common facilities and entry points such as mobile sites and government app stores.

M-government may further transcend the traditional e-government service delivery model, by bringing personalized, localized and context-aware services to its citizens. Mobile technology allows information to support the service directly where the customer is located, taking service close to the public to be served. In the process, it transforms governance, making it more fluid, and capable of providing immediate, responsive, and localized service.

M-government is best suited for the developing world, which has low access to computers, but has almost ubiquitous mobile penetration. To take full advantage of the mobile platform, a priority list of high-impact m-services and a longer list of "quick wins" can be developed for rapid implementation by the government, especially at the municipal level.

A holistic strategy for transformation, integrating mobile with other aspects of e-government, can help identify crucial gaps in the applications development ecosystem and open up opportunities for partnering with civil society and the private sector. Leadership from the private sector, academia, and nongovernment agencies is essential for sustainable transformation, since innovations in mobile applications and services mostly come from these sources. Public-private and multi-stakeholder partnerships will be particularly critical for innovation and cost-effective delivery of m-services.

M-government needs to be an integral part of broader reform initiatives. So far, most of m-government initiatives have come from isolated bottom-up efforts. This is changing and best practices that adopt government-wide approaches are emerging. The essential ingredients of digital government and mobile government are indistinguishable, as are the major policy concerns of security, interoperability, privacy, information quality, human capacity, or financial sustainability. These issues are best addressed jointly at the national level.

Tap big data and analytics

Government transformed with the help of analytics and big data is a "government by design": a more disciplined, systematic approach to solving public-sector management problems through granular and timely data and analyses. Figure 5 describes the sources and uses of big data.

Breakthroughs in data-capturing technologies, geo-mapping, open source mobile apps, social media, data standards and storage, visualization, analytic tools, and optimization sciences have created opportunities for fact-based decision making and fast-learning cycles. Of particular interest are data sources such as online and mobile financial transactions, social media, and GPS coordinates, which are growing at astronomical rates. For example, the growth of mobile data traffic from emerging markets has exceeded 100 percent annually. Mobile data, spanning a huge population even in low-income countries, help service providers understand client behavior, and enable user-centric solutions among others in areas as diverse as education, health, finance, and agriculture. To turn mobile data into a government transformation tool, a number of ecosystem elements must be put in place—privacy and security for users, and incentives for government, civil society, and private sector to share and use data for the benefit of society.

What can big data and analytics offer as part of government transformation?

* Drive transparency and accountability, and detect fraud.
* Improve understanding of organizational performance and program results.

Figure 5: Sources and Uses of Big Data

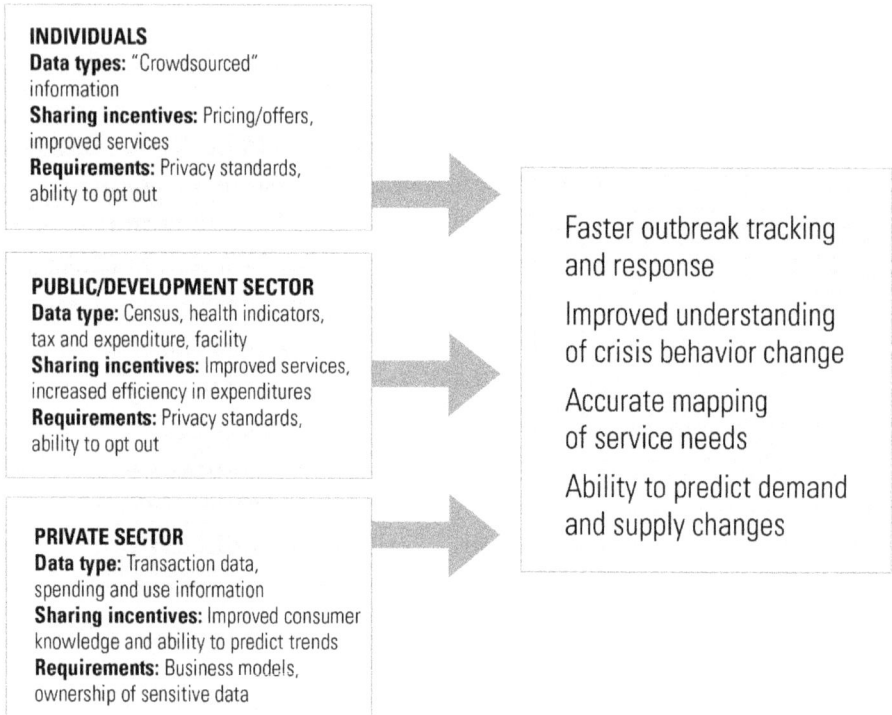

INDIVIDUALS
Data types: "Crowdsourced" information
Sharing incentives: Pricing/offers, improved services
Requirements: Privacy standards, ability to opt out

PUBLIC/DEVELOPMENT SECTOR
Data type: Census, health indicators, tax and expenditure, facility
Sharing incentives: Improved services, increased efficiency in expenditures
Requirements: Privacy standards, ability to opt out

PRIVATE SECTOR
Data type: Transaction data, spending and use information
Sharing incentives: Improved consumer knowledge and ability to predict trends
Requirements: Business models, ownership of sensitive data

Faster outbreak tracking and response

Improved understanding of crisis behavior change

Accurate mapping of service needs

Ability to predict demand and supply changes

Source: World Economic Forum, 2012

- Enable piloting and experimentation to discover needs, explore linkages (e.g., between sanitation, water supply, and health).
- Improve understanding of the poor. Development economists are increasingly aware of their limited understanding of poverty, and how to respond to the needs of the poor in cost-effective ways (Banarjee and Duflo, 2011).

- Improve customization of public services, based on segmentation, locational information, and evidence of citizen needs and behaviors.[14]
- Create new services and business models, based on sharing and analyzing timely and granular data from public and private services providers.
- Map status and location of services and needs, for advocacy, systems planning, and service improvement, particularly in unmapped poor communities.
- Improve feedback from citizens on policies and from users on services.
- Research complex systems via modeling and simulation, to unearth valuable insights for policymaking, infrastructure usage, and urban systems management.
- Drive smarter decisions through evidence-based policy, using Decision Support Systems (DSS), predictive analytics, and anticipatory problem detection.
- Provide early warning and real-time surveillance and feedback, participatory sensing, and local impact tracking, as in natural disasters or disease outbreaks.

What are the challenges to adopting big data and analytics in government?

- Low awareness by policy makers of the potential (and limitations) of big data/analytics for development, leading to weak demand and impact.
- Low awareness of the availability of big data and analytics tools—wasting resources through duplication.

---

14 See, for example, anonymized locational data in Ivory Coast that provided valuable insights for designing public services including public transportation. Similarly the Harvard School of Public Health has demonstrated the use of locational data for malaria tracking in Kenya.

- Limited local capacity to make analytics technologies relevant.[15]
- Weak links between software apps developers, sector specialists, and potential users (underdeveloped ecosystem).
- Poor data quality, standards, and interoperability, and the need for resources and systems to manage and share data effectively.
- Uncertain, unbalanced, or weak data privacy and security policies and intellectual property rights.
- Shortage of skilled analysts, data-driven managers and policy makers—most acute in governments.
- Poor understanding of local context: misinterpreting data and correlations—the challenge of developing sophisticated users of information.
- Excessive technology hype and supply push without due attention to policies, institutions, and skills necessary to sustain big data interventions.
- Weak incentives and structures to support the sharing and use of data, leading to limited access to government and service provider data.
- Poor technology infrastructure.

Given these challenges, it is critical to strengthen relationships among various actors of the ecosystem, and prioritize and sequence steps to manage big data analytics for public policy and program management (Figure 6). Government can catalyze the development of this ecosystem through the opening of its own datasets and active management of use and dissemination. Policy makers can set the legal frameworks governing data privacy and security, establish data commons, and incentivize public agencies to continually improve the data they make available.

---

15 For a good example of new intermediaries with the requisite skills to help client organizations exploit analytics technologies and gain insights into their businesses see Singapore's Business Analytics Translational Center.

A public agency may take these steps to build or expand the use of big-data analytics:

- Establish shared understanding of goals and perspectives and how they are being measured. Communicate how data will be used in decision-making and program management, and how analytics will aid in transformation.
- Prepare leadership to support decision-making, performance management, and managerial innovation. Secure their ownership, fight complacency, and seek change from business as usual.
- Engage stakeholders early, particularly those representing the demand side. Build communities of practice.

Figure 6: The Big Data Ecosystem

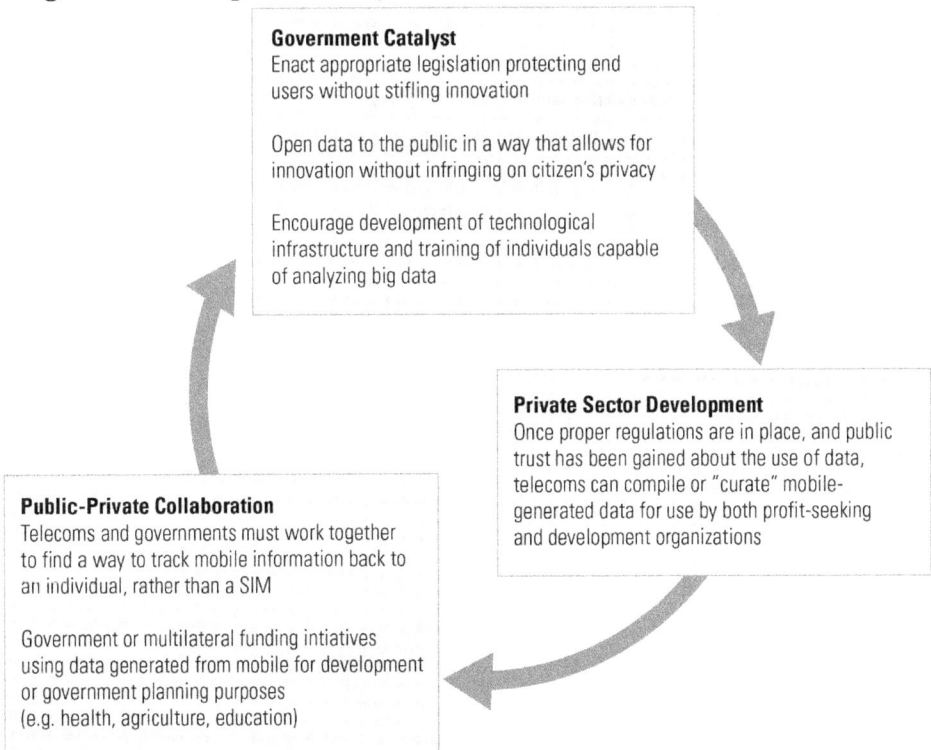

Government Catalyst
Enact appropriate legislation protecting end users without stifling innovation

Open data to the public in a way that allows for innovation without infringing on citizen's privacy

Encourage development of technological infrastructure and training of individuals capable of analyzing big data

Private Sector Development
Once proper regulations are in place, and public trust has been gained about the use of data, telecoms can compile or "curate" mobile-generated data for use by both profit-seeking and development organizations

Public-Private Collaboration
Telecoms and governments must work together to find a way to track mobile information back to an individual, rather than a SIM

Government or multilateral funding intiatives using data generated from mobile for development or government planning purposes
(e.g. health, agriculture, education)

Source: World Economic Forum, 2012

- Take a whole-of-government approach to analytics to encourage partnerships within agencies, with other agencies, and with key partners and stakeholders outside government.

- Embed analytics in key government sectors such as finance and tax administration—in the United States, this is pioneered by the OMB.

- Assess capabilities, and create a cadre of analysts. Ask what incentives are in place and nurture analytical talents in the public sector. Complement skills via public-private partnerships.

- Give priority to performance metrics, dashboards, and scorecards, and establish measurements that support the agency's strategic goals.

- Be demand driven: understand beneficiaries of services, key performance problems to solve, etc.

- Create a culture of measurement, and analytics. Ask questions even if they cannot be answered with current data: What should be measured? What are we doing to achieve results?

- Create platforms for data sharing, and for others to build tools and applications. Share and consolidate data across agencies, assess impact on multiple agencies.

- Leverage mobile phones as an easy-to-use and ubiquitous platform for generating, disseminating, and using big data analytics.

- Encourage doing things differently and doing different things that were not possible to do before the advent of big data analytics.

- Chunk initial analytics to demonstrate their value and use outcomes to inform next steps. An incremental approach may show benefits rapidly and allow for testing the process.

- Take a long-term view of empowering public agencies with big data and analytics. It is a learning process.[16]

---

16 A number of assessment tools are emerging for analytical capabilities. See for example Davenport and Jarvenpaa (2008).

CREATE ECOSYSTEMS FOR OPEN GOVERNMENT DATA (OGD)

Part of an emerging culture of disclosure and transparency and a recent global movement, OGD makes public sector data technically and legally open for use.[17] Along with big data and analytics, it is providing visibility and access to an unprecedented amount of information about government, business, and population.

Because of its socio-economic benefits, OGD initiatives are spreading across the world at all levels of government.[18] Early examples from the United States and the United Kingdom were studied for their contribution and applicability to the developing world.[19] In 2011, Kenya became the first country in sub-Saharan Africa to follow in their footsteps with the Kenya Open Government Data Portal.[20]

OGD is believed to improve accountability of public agencies while strengthening citizen participation and, along the way, allow users to create, or even co-create, economic value from public sector information. As governments engage in the open data ecosystem, they are pressured to transform and innovate their own practices and services.

OGD, therefore, propels innovation in data-generated services, increases efficiency of existing services, and improves governance, policy-making and decision-making. Recent data from the European Community suggest that OGD policies can increase European business activity by up to EUR 40 billion annually (EC, 2011). The potential economic benefit from open data (from governments as well as business) is estimated to be $ 3 trillion (McKinsey Global Institute, 2011).

Although it comes with much promise, OGD also come with limitations. The World Economic Forum, for example, has noted that the balance between OGD and information security is an ongoing concern for

17 http://www.opengovdata.org

18 See, for example, US: http://www.whitehouse.gov/open and Australia: http://www. finance.gov.au/e-government/strategy-and-governance/gov2/declaration-of-open-government.html

19 US: data.gov and the UK: data.gov.uk

20 https://opendata.go.ke

public officials, one that is likely to get more scrutiny as these initiatives continue to evolve (WEF, 2011a).

Many factors influence the pace and magnitude of realizing the benefits of the open data ecosystem. OGD is not just about opening the digital data stores of government. It demands the development of open government policies, laws, skills, leadership, and culture, and citizen engagement through various forums. It calls for supply-side as well as demand-side measures. Promoting citizen engagement without associated ICT-enabled reforms and change management within governments may run the risks of raising unrealistic expectations and fanning discontent. OGD can thrive only through partnerships between public agencies, application and content developers, and civil society organizations, creating a vibrant open-data ecosystem. It takes time to realize the benefits of OGD, often five years or longer, and informational capabilities of citizens and poor communities, among other factors, can severely limit the benefits.

Policy makers should develop policies and institutions to support the evolution of the entire OGD ecosystem. The United States adopted the "open by design" principle—an open government data policy. The federal government also created new posts of chief data officers in the federal agencies. A structured dialogue among public agencies (major suppliers of OGD) and the major users is increasingly used to understand the demand side and prioritize the openness of federal datasets. Other countries too are developing national institutions to promote OGD. The United Kingdom has an Open Data Institute (ODI) project conceived to encourage governments, individuals, companies, groups and organizations to be more open with the data they control.

Developing countries should give special attention to the demand side of their OGD ecosystem—the enabling environment and capacity for the use of data. Supply-side measures for easy access to data require establishing the right data quality, data standards, and data-sharing technology. To create a thriving OGD ecosystem, awareness and culture for OGD is critical. Building analytical and data management capabilities within user agencies can maximize the economic value of OGD, strengthen demand, and help create new businesses and intermediaries that can drive more value from national data resources. Emerging global best practices include proactive disclosure of existing digital data on the web, the creation of a negative list of information that may not be shared, and the setting of a timeline to ensure that there is regular disclosure of government records and other information.

More ambitious steps in the move toward OGD include information policy that deals comprehensively with best practices in information collection, storage, retrieval, and management at the national level, and technology policy that mandates the use of open standards in e-government to promote interoperability and prevent vendor lock-in, with only temporary and limited exceptions. All information should be provided free of cost. Public outreach and citizen-oriented tools will ensure a vibrant public sphere, both online and offline, where government data are used and discussed and a feedback loop is created. Social media integration will allow governments to leverage network effects and defray costs. There also should be a single-point portal to provide access to different public authorities' data. Finally, all data should be cloud based to lower government overhead costs.

Collaboration among countries is extended beyond sharing best practices to building open source tools and platforms for open government data, and beyond traditional North-South transfer to joint initiatives and South-South sharing. A promising example is a joint initiative of the United States and India. The OGD Platform India—data.gov.in—is intended for use by the Government of India to publish datasets, documents, services, tools and applications, increase transparency in the functioning of government, and open avenues for more innovative uses of government data. The platform is also packaged as a product and made available in open source for implementation by countries globally. The entire product is available for download at thopen source code-sharing platform "GitHub."

How should we measure progress on open data? One such scheme encourages governments to publish their data, awarding points for availability, structure, nonproprietary, identification for reuse and linking to other data to provide context. It is also possible to measure government interest in such initiatives. For example, are the legal foundations for open information in place and are they listed on government website?[21]

The World Bank, in collaboration with other partners, has developed an open government data tool kit.[22] It provides learning resources, selected institutions (like OGP) and communities of practice, and sources for technical assistance and finance for open data initiatives in developing countries. It also offers suggestions on technology options, how to manage supply and quality of data, and how to build demand and engagement. One readiness assessment tool is a promising work-in progress being piloted in a number of countries.[23] It provides a structured set of questions to help assess readiness along key dimensions.

The US federal government has made the Data.gov website, the central repository of federal open data, accessible and useful. The Digital Accountability and Transparency Act (DATA) is expected to bring transparency of government spending to new levels of detail. Legislative proposals aim to modernize the Freedom of Information Act (FOIA) and make more information requests available as open data. The federal Challenge.gov website applies the best principles of crowdsourcing and collective intelligence: it poses challenges using the government's open data resources to solve national or agency problems (J. Gurin, 2013).

This is the path to a vibrant OGD ecosystem where government data will be truly impactful through a process of continuous interplay between data supply, usage, and feedback, leading to continuous improvement of data quality and usefulness.

---

21 http://www.opengovpartnership.org

22 http://data.worldbank.org/about/open-government-data-toolkit/knowledge-repository

23 http://data.worldbank.org/about/open-government-data-toolkit/readiness-assessment-tool

Transforming Key Sectors

———

CATALYZE SECTORAL ECOSYSTEMS

Many factors that drive sector transformation are no different from those required for transforming government (Chapter 4). Basic among them are a shared vision of the future; support to sector policy reforms; continuous assessment of performance management and service delivery; and systematic dealing with barriers to adoption and readiness for e-transformation.

A sector transformation strategy will benefit from taking an ecosystem view of the target sector (demand or ICT user), combined with a holistic view of the ICT ecosystem (supply or enabler). Such a view would start by mapping the possible interactions within and between the two ecosystems. Ultimately it is the quality and strength of these interactions that will determine the speed, effectiveness, and sustainability of sector transformation. The government plays a dual role in shaping these interactions: as policy and rule maker to create the enabling environment, and as a strategic investor in ICT applications and data in support of transformation of the target sector.

Mapping key elements in each ecosystem, their stakeholders, and their interactions can help focus attention on these elements without losing sight of the broader picture. It can also identify the foundational blocks and enablers, facilitate policy coherence, and reinforce innovations that can move the whole sector toward sustainable transformation.

BUILD A VISION-DRIVEN TRANSFORMATION STRATEGY

It is a common pitfall to view ICT as a short-term technological enhancement, rather than a deep socio-technical transformation. A second pitfall is to commit to ICT investments that are not in sync with the sector's reform strategy and thus ignore the incentive system and the needed investment in complementary skills and organizational changes. A third is to proceed with major ICT investments without a shared vision for the future. Finally, a fourth is excessive reliance on a single ICT tool (often the latest fad or the next new thing) without deploying other elements of the ecosystem. All of these are avoidable, but frequent in practice, leading to high levels of failure in meeting transformational objectives. Alternatively, they create islands of innovation and isolated best practices, but fail to diffuse and scale, or lead to sector-wide step change and impact.

To realize the transformative potential of ICT, digital transformation must be guided by a clear vision of the sector, appreciation of current challenges and future opportunities, and substantive policy reform. Sector leaders should communicate at all levels a well articulated shared vision. An energizing vision will motivate key stakeholders, initiate coherent reforms, facilitate partnerships, mobilize resources for strategic investments in ICT and complementary assets, and commit management to sustained change efforts.

Transformational technology leaders, including chief information officers (CIOs), should engage in this process, to understand the demand side and inform other executives of what is realistically possible with the new technologies, as well as the best practices that can be transferred from other sectors or countries. ICT leaders and target sector leaders must be creatively engaged so that the intended reforms for the target sector can drive ICT-enabled transformations. At the same time, ICT leaders would open up possibilities for innovations, new services, and new paths to transformation.

Readiness assessments and benchmarking are useful tools to apply to sector-level transformation, as much as they are useful for transforming government or the whole economy (see Chapters 3, 4). Assessment should cover sector leadership, political economy of the sector, and incentives and organizational structures needed to support digital transformation. It would also include ICT skills and resources of the sector, existing online services and digital data, and connectivity and shared communication infrastructure. In addition to e-readiness, vision development and transformation priorities of a targeted sector will benefit from comparator indicators of sector performance and outcome, as in comparative costs of health services and educational achievements across countries, and among cities and regions of a country. Such contextual understanding of the sector and its performance challenges is at least as critical as assessing its e-readiness in order to guide transformational priorities.

The remaining part of this chapter illustrates this holistic approach to sector transformation in education and financial services sectors.

TRANSFORM EDUCATION AND LEARNING SYSTEMS

Imperatives for transforming education. Globalization and the ICT revolution are raising the demand for, and changing the nature of, education and learning. The networked society requires new expertise: digital and technological literacy, communication skills, problem solving, critical thinking, self-learning, teamwork, change management, creativity, and initiative. Understanding this interplay at a relatively detailed level is critical to leveraging this technology for educational reforms.

With accelerated technological change, growing premium for educated and skilled manpower, and new channels for knowledge, a culture of continuous learning is essential for a networked society. Education systems must shift from textbook knowledge to teaching how to learn and become agile problem solvers. Much of this learning must occur through networks that cut across academic, business, local, and global communities. Digital communication, open source content, social networking, and collaboration technologies further enable the creation and dynamism of these learning systems. The technological revolution appears central to learning today, and will change how education services are delivered. The knowledge revolution places further demands on educational institutions, to modernize curriculum at all levels, to integrate digital tools and the Internet into learning and professional development, and to prepare young people for lifelong learning. Where universities used to educate only a tiny elite, they must now train and retrain increasing numbers of learners throughout their careers.

Yet, educational systems in many countries are in organizational and financial crisis. Governments are unable to subsidize universities as generously as they used to, even in affluent countries like the United States. Public officials, businesspeople, families, and workers are struggling to finance increases in the coverage, quality, and duration of education. Only ICT-enabled transformation can meet these challenges adequately and continue to scale up education for the future.

Role of ICT in transforming education. The role of ICT is increasingly evident in higher education. Countries are under pressure to reform their higher education systems, to develop open systems that recognize prior experience and exchange schemes, and to establish lifelong learning frameworks. Universities are called upon to collaborate with public and private sectors to contribute to innovation and tap global and local knowledge. New competition, modes of operation, and forms of delivery are emerging in higher education and corporate training, including distance education, mixed-mode teaching, open online universities, mega and virtual universities, corporate universities, and various forms of private sector participation and borderless educational services. Digital or online education promises to reinvent higher education. Its fundamental elements are connectivity, knowledge management, education technology, and partnership. In turn, digital education raises new demands for transforming governance and management of educational systems along with flexibility, quality assurance, and industry linkages.

At a more basic level, ICT can effectively contain the increasing costs of education. Without the redesign of education systems with greater use of ICT, whose relative price is falling, the price of conventional education will become prohibitive in many countries. Meanwhile productivity in this sector is diminishing, stagnant, or at best increasing at a glacial pace. Consequently, the relative price of education continues to rise.

Competition among providers of education and training services will be crucial to technology-enhanced learning. The private sector has a comparative advantage in introducing technology to workers as it has the required flexibility, agility, and responsiveness to provide just-in-time training. It could also partner with governments and engage in "education on demand," to help spur the provision of timely learning for business and society.

There are several rationales for leveraging and mainstreaming ICT in general education and training as well. The most important rationale is pedagogical: ICT offers enormous potential for enhancing access and quality of education and training, and can help shift the focus from teaching to learning, from teacher-centered education to learner-centered and learner-paced systems. Next comes a social or equity rationale: as ICT is now pervasive in everyday life, integrating ICT in education would level the playing field, familiarize young students early with digital networks and tools, and start them on a lifelong journey of learning and discovery. Then there is the employment and vocational rationale: ICT-based skills such as networking skills, IT-enabled services, desktop publishing, etc. are required for today's new job market. Finally, there is the catalytic rationale: ICT accelerates reforms in teaching as well as in education management.

ICT is expanding access to education via distance education, digital learning, and lifelong learning for workers, and supporting communities of practice for teachers.[24] In many African countries, simple mobile apps are used for monitoring schools, teachers, and student performance, including attendance.[25] In India, cloud schools (without teachers) are being piloted to offer a new education channel for the

---

24 Portal SouthAfrica.info

25 Thutong: SA's education portal, 2012

poor in the remotest areas (*The Economist*, 2013a). ICT-enabled functional literacy programs are piloted for disadvantaged women in West Bengal (ITU, 2013b). Smart school networks are being built to integrate ICT literacy and ICT-aided learning into primary schools and their surrounding communities in Egypt (UNDP, 2007). In Rwanda, educational information is captured directly from schools into databases and used to improve educational administration and policy making (World Bank, 2011).

A promising model of the use of ICT in education and poverty alleviation is Connect To Learn, an expanding coalition of public, private, and nonprofit partners and contributors in support of secondary education for all.[26] Ericsson and Columbia University, among others, have partnered to use ICT to enable children in poor African villages to complete high school. "Connect to Learn" classrooms are equipped with online educational materials that can provide a world of information in schools that have few, if any, books. As Jeffrey Sachs put it, "Just as rural communities have leapfrogged banking by making payments on mobile phones, so, too, these communities could use technology to leapfrog ahead in education" (*Washington Post*, June 23, 2014, p. A15).

In Brazil, a nongovernmental organization (NGO) is helping communities to develop "information technology and citizenship schools." Communities that meet the sustainability criteria are provided with technical assistance and training for instructors as well as help to procure and install initial donation of hardware. More than 35,000 Brazilian children in over 200 schools in 30 cities have been trained in basic computer literacy. In Chile, 5000 basic and secondary schools received computers and education software, along with training and ongoing support from a technical assistance network of 35 universities organized by the ministry of education. In South Africa, School Net provides Internet services to local schools, including connectivity and technical support. The challenges of scaling up the impact of such pilots have been substantial. A national ICT strategy must build on such experiences to increase

---

26 http://connecttolearn.org/about-us/Partners

coverage and effectiveness. Pilots are necessary but not sufficient. It is good to remember that comprehensive reform should be built on what has been proven to work.

Key lessons. Despite substantial resources being invested in technological transformation, experience points to an apparent disconnect between the rationales presented to advance the use of ICT and their actual use (Turcano, 2005). While the rhetoric is about changing the teaching-learning paradigm, actual programs of ICT in education predominantly offer computer literacy and dissemination of digital learning materials. In practice, therefore, ICT is used to support existing teaching and learning practices with new and often expensive tools. The challenge is to bridge this disconnect. Lessons that emerged were not always widely disseminated or made accessible to policy makers in developing countries. Little documentation exists about scaling up of pilots and innovative use of ICT in education, while there are many pitfalls involved in e-education strategy implementation. An enduring one, for example, is putting technology before education—a typical bias toward hardware and connectivity issues, with little attention to relevant content and teacher training.

Having local capabilities in ICT and a thriving ICT industry is no guarantee for mastering the use of ICT in the education sector. A study in South Asia (InfoDev and PriceWaterhouseCoopers, 2010) indicates proliferation of ICT tools at all levels of education. With the success of the IT industry in that region, ICT is used enthusiastically, often without real understanding of their relevance, interdependencies and impact. Initiatives are planned in isolation and without a proper policy framework.

Here are some guidelines that will help to systematically integrate lessons learned into transformational plans for education (adapted from Turcano, 2005).

- ***Promote a comprehensive approach***. Access alone is not enough to create a cultural shift toward ICT use. All elements—hardware, software, Internet access, teacher incentives and training, improved pedagogy, high quality online content and educational software—have to come together in a school at the same time.

- *Build a critical mass of trained teachers.* Provide incentives to teachers and administrations. In Chile, it was found at least 60 percent of teachers in the same school had to receive training at the same time to create a cultural shift in the school toward ICT. Training one teacher per school is a waste of money.

- *Train teachers in new pedagogical practices.* Help create more learner-centric pedagogical environment enabled by ICT. Technical ICT skills are necessary but not sufficient for successful integration of ICT into teaching. Development of appropriate pedagogical practices is more important.

- *Continually expose teachers to ICT.* To remain current and select appropriate resources, teachers must know about fast emerging applications. Experience shows that even in advanced countries, few teachers have comprehensive knowledge of the range of ICT tools and resources for education.

- *Create a compelling ICT environment.* Promote use of ICT in administration functions and link knowledge of ICT to future promotion for teachers.

- *Seek cost effective, sustainable ICT solutions.* Maintenance, operational support and constant upgrading of ICT can be costly. Public-private partnerships should be mobilized and evaluated. Alternatives such as Free and Open Source Software (FOSS) may greatly reduce the cost of software procurement.

- *Seek innovative approaches to content development.* Digitizing content is a lengthy and expensive process, especially for educational television and video production. Lack of digital educational content directly related to the curriculum and absence of assessment of outcomes can be important barriers to successful transformation efforts in education.

* ***Build partnerships with the private sector and academia.***
Collaboration with the private sector helps develop effective educational software, relevant content and training programs. Academic partnerships help to improve teacher education and develop a network of trainers.

Adopting an ecosystem view (Figure 7). Education systems around the world are resistant to change. Systemic changes require mutually reinforcing policies, incentives and investments. Effective ICT adoption with transformative outcomes requires detailed planning at every level. It means revamping policy, strategy, program management, communication, monitoring and evaluation, knowledge creation, and sharing mechanisms. It also requires enhanced connectivity, digital and open source content development, access to educational portals, networked communities of practice, and dynamic curriculum development. A transformational education strategy must be guided by a holistic vision of the needs of the sector, aligned with the national strategy, and driven by clear pedagogical philosophies. Unfortunately, this approach is challenged by the fact that in many countries different parts of government are responsible for ICT in education, with no mechanism for coordination. Yet, successful transformation demands inputs from many players: ministries of education, labor, ICT, science and technology, finance, and rural development, as well as academic institutions, NGOs, civil society, media, and the private sector.

Figure 7: The E-education Ecosystem

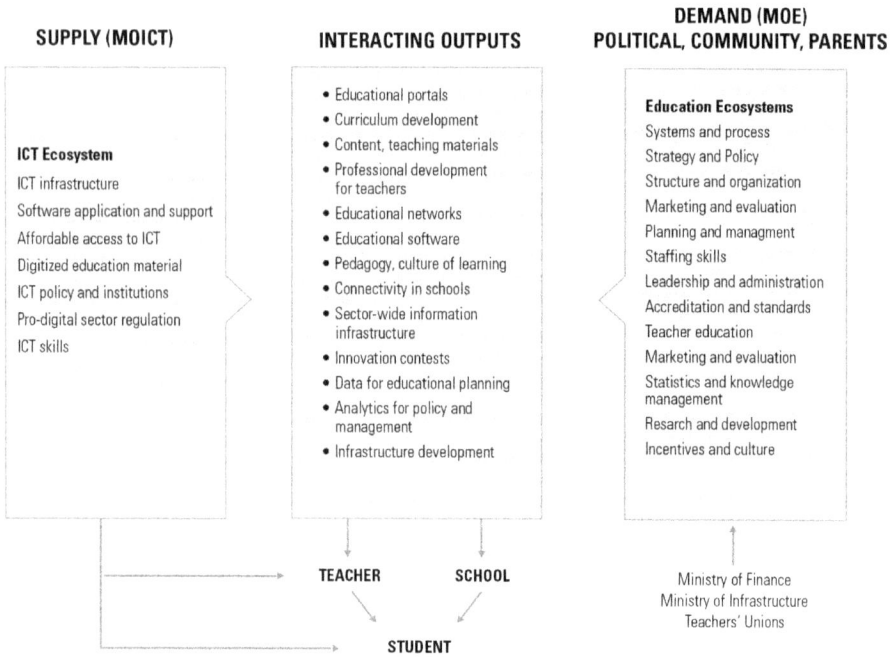

SUPPLY (MOICT)	INTERACTING OUTPUTS	DEMAND (MOE) POLITICAL, COMMUNITY, PARENTS
ICT Ecosystem ICT infrastructure Software application and support Affordable access to ICT Digitized education material ICT policy and institutions Pro-digital sector regulation ICT skills	• Educational portals • Curriculum development • Content, teaching materials • Professional development for teachers • Educational networks • Educational software • Pedagogy, culture of learning • Connectivity in schools • Sector-wide information infrastructure • Innovation contests • Data for educational planning • Analytics for policy and management • Infrastructure development	**Education Ecosystems** Systems and process Strategy and Policy Structure and organization Marketing and evaluation Planning and managment Staffing skills Leadership and administration Accreditation and standards Teacher education Marketing and evaluation Statistics and knowledge management Resarch and development Incentives and culture

TEACHER   SCHOOL

Ministry of Finance
Ministry of Infrastructure
Teachers' Unions

STUDENT

MOICT: Ministry of ICT
MOE: Ministry of Education
Source: Author

Transformational leaders should ask: which problem in education does ICT address? How does ICT improve the learning process and teaching practices? What changes in incentives, skills, and support mechanisms will be necessary to move from access to ICT tools to access to relevant content and knowledge, and to actual changes in teaching and learning processes? What kinds of accreditation systems, account-ability, and safeguards will be needed to adopt, and realize the promise of, a massive open online course (MOOC) education? What educational policies and regulations would facilitate the "creative destruction" that digital education promises to bring about?

ICT-enabled transformation must also revamp antiquated educational administration, and record management systems. Mobile tools can feed data concerning student and teacher attendance—a major problem in developing countries. They can help stakeholders and communities monitor budgets, monitor school construction, provide access to textbooks, and identify sources of corruption. Educational governance, performance management, and policymaking can be transformed with real time data, big data, analytics, digital records, multiple feedback loops, and mobile monitoring. Investment in and experimentation with big data are spreading in the advanced countries; but these tools may have even more impact on education in developing countries.

The future of online and personalized education. Learning is an active process in which people construct new understandings of the world around them through exploration, experimentation, and discussion. ICT is the new medium through which people can simulate, create, express and interact. For example, children can now use computer simulations to explore the workings of systems of the world, from natural ecosystems to economic systems to immune systems. The Internet and distance learning are expanding the learning ecosystem beyond schools, enabling new types of "knowledge building communities" in which children and adults around the world collaborate on projects and learn from each other. The possibilities for using ICT to transform learning are enormous, teaching learners how to locate information, judge credibility of the sources, engage in collaborative problem solving, and take ownership of how and what they learn. Text no longer has to be the main medium for conveying meaning, as interactive multimedia can more effectively develop understanding. Curricula can incorporate projects that call for mixed sets of skills and backgrounds, enabling networked learning and learning communities.

Other exciting possibilities include the ability to capture information and provide feedback in real time. Mass education can shift toward personalized learning. Teaching programs can monitor children's progress and the data derived can be used to tailor what the child confronts on the computer screen. In the school of tomorrow, teachers become learning companions; they accompany students on their learning journey. The borders between home and school may disappear. Digital textbooks are multi-dimensionally richer than print, as they enable students to visualize and simulate, link to other sources, join forums and search for data. Tablets are made for active and collaborative learning: they enable students worldwide to meet in web-based forums to create databases, wikis, image boards, and other resources. Tablets also give access to games, virtual worlds, and various group learning. Schools may well become community-learning hubs, while knowledge is increasingly constructed in collaboration among learners (Slinger, 2004).

Ubiquitous connectivity and mobile technology will also enable high-quality global education. The open-source movement will allow students to access the lectures of top college professors (see MIT's OpenCourseWare program). Mobile technology will open the door to remote, effective, and less costly instruction. If appropriate policies are adopted to allow for national and global competition in education services, mobile devices and ubiquitous connectivity can broaden markets, push for swift change, and shatter the incumbents (Saylor, 2013).

MOOC is a hugely disruptive mode of education services delivery. Its promise is being exploited in the United States, the United Kingdom, the European Union, and to a lesser extent in developing countries. Elite universities like Harvard, MIT, and Stanford are pioneering MOOC delivery. Major traditional educational institutions are beginning to offer full MOOC degree programs. In Brazil, Unopar University offers low-cost yet relatively high-quality degree courses using online materials and weekly seminars, reaching many rural towns and working people throughout the country. With low start-up costs and powerful economies of scale, MOOC is likely to spread to countries where there is a massive need to be met with a fast growing cohort of university population. Education and ICT policy makers should leverage this opportunity and its implications for all levels of the education ecosystem.

Online learning often has high dropout rates, and uncertain quality of service. MOOC providers currently make most of their money from the certificates they grant to students, and maintaining a reasonable completion rate is important for financial viability. However, ensuring transparency and quality and safeguarding the consumer are important for digital education to succeed. Policy makers, therefore, should secure the necessary regulatory environment for MOOC.

Transform finance

Worldwide, about 50 percent of adults are unbanked. In Africa the figure is 80 percent. In India, less than 2 percent of the population possesses a credit card (World Bank, 2012). The fundamental problem is transaction costs, and it is not the poor alone who are impacted. Businessmen turn to more costly ways to borrow. Credit moves sluggishly or not at all across whole economies. Micro finance institutions such as Grameen Bank, have only partly solved the transaction costs problem. In this environment, the mobile phone offers an easy, fast and very low-cost channel to move digital cash and drive credit. Developing countries stand to benefit faster from such innovation, perhaps far more than from foreign aid.

Mobile-based financial tools have the potential to dramatically lower the costs of delivering financial services to the poor around the world. Mobile platforms link banks to clients in real time, enabling banks to instantly relay account information, send regular remittances, or send reminders for payments due—encouraging saving and financial discipline. Mobile money systems can also serve as a platform for additional innovations and apps, from paying bills electronically to avoiding lengthy queue times, to applying for short-term loans, to securing efficient conditional cash transfers for drought relief, educating girls, or other emergency transfers and compensation schemes. Clients can sign up for services quickly on their own. Moreover, mobile communications generates huge amounts of data, which banks and other service providers can use to understand the behavior and needs of various groups and develop profitable, responsive services.

M-Pesa, Kenya's mobile-based money transfer system was launched in 2007. By 2012 it was used by over 17 million Kenyans, two-thirds of the adult population. About 25 percent of the country's gross national product flows through it. M-Pesa has since been extended to offer loans and savings products, and to disburse salaries and pay bills, saving users further time and money. For rural Kenyan households that adopted M-Pesa, incomes increased by 5–30 percent (Morawczynski, 2010). The availability of a reliable mobile payments platform has spawned a host of start-ups in Nairobi, whose business models build on M-Pesa's foundations. More recently, M-Pesa has been diffused to 45 percent of Tanzania. Going global, it has been adopted in 72 countries, with the potential to cover 2 billion people with cell phones but no bank account (*The Economist,* 2013b).

Financial and insurance services too are being built on the M-Pesa platform. For example, the Kilimo Salama scheme (Swahili for "safe farming," launched in 2010) is a mobile micro-insurance service that grants weather-indexed insurance to small farmers. This product was developed between several enterprises, a public agri-business company, a mobile phone operator, an insurance company, and the Kenyan Meteorological Department. Every time a farmer buys seeds, fertilizer or other agro-chemicals, he or she can also buy insurance against weather unfavorable to the crops. In case of crop failure due to drought or excessive rain, insured farmers are entitled to compensatory payments through M-Pesa. Clients are hooked up to a local computerized weather station, and payments are automatically linked to rainfall. No one has to file a claim, and the payment goes directly to the farmer's M-Pesa account. Within a month of its launch, 9,500 farmers subscribed to the weather index insurance scheme.[27]

In India, ICT provides low-cost platforms for branchless banking and microfinance, and instant financial transactions. Eko India leverages existing retail shops, mobile networks, and banks to extend branchless banking services and offer payment, cash collection, and disbursal services. Users employ handheld devices to open accounts and send money to people and places around the country. Low-cost smart cards have been piloted in Andhra Pradesh, to improve access to microfinance. Smart cards with embedded microchips containing information on clients' credit histories are helping SKS Microfinance to reduce transaction costs. Smart cards have been identified as a solution to the high cost of delivery, because they can lead to gains in efficiency, eliminate paperwork, reduce errors, and fraud. Potential savings in operations are estimated to be around 18 percent (Cecchini and Scott, 2003).

The case for an ecosystem approach. Mobile money innovations exist at the intersection of finance, ICT, and the target (sector, beneficiary group, country) that needs to be transformed. Private sector players come from different fields: network operators, banks, payment card firms, and supporting businesses and agents. Success of mobile money will depend on the overall status of the finance and mobile industries. Commitment of leading firms can drive adoption, but already existing alternatives or small market size can limit the economies of scale. Understanding end users is also essential to creating a trustworthy value proposition that fits the social context.

Government plays a significant role in creating an enabling environment with appropriate regulations for both finance and ICT, and for privacy and security. Regulatory attention is needed to ensure appropriate competition and interoperability. The form of competition will depend on context (World Bank, 2012). Similarly, governments influence access and scale via their universal access policies and programs (Chapter 8). Since mobile money services manage the limited capital of

---

27 UNCTAD, 2010 (page 71).

the poor, safeguards for consumer protection are essential. Successful regulation is marked by collaboration between telecom and finance industry, government, and civil society.

The transformation of financial services via mobile devices is still at an early stage in the world and faces many challenges (CGAP, 2011). The pioneering model of M-Pesa has been widely replicated but may not fit well in other contexts, for example, where an extensive ATM network is in place as in Thailand. Technological trends will also influence the evolution and range of mobile money applications: smartphones, near field communications, and biometrics. A product gap exists in many countries between the financial services offered and those wanted by the poor. Simply formalizing people's finances onto a mobile platform falls short of meaningful financial inclusion. The transformational potential of mobile money models will be realized when finance is extended to the unbanked populations and tailored products and services enable the majority of world population to better manage their assets (World Bank, 2012).

Part Three: Mastering the Implementation of Digital Transformation

———

Mastering the digital transformation process demands developing specialized leadership and institutional capabilities, enacting digital economy policies and regulations, investing in high quality and dynamic communication infrastructure, and building local capacity for agile implementation and fast learning from local and global practice. These are the subjects of the next four chapters.

CHAPTER 6

Developing Leadership and Institutions

———

Stable and informed leadership is important to adopting long-term strategies and sustainable policies for nations and institutions. Leaders are expected to manage the change that accompanies transformation; but first and foremost, they need to define the roles of government, private sectors, and other development partners.

Leaders motivate followers with visions of the future. They communicate why transformation matters. They bridge sectoral boundaries, and coordinate across institutions to set policies, overcome political and bureaucratic barriers, and manage structural change. They create learning communities of practice. Leaders build and rely on institutions with requisite core competencies for program management and implementation. Institutions leading e-transformation strategies are at the heart of the transformation process. They engage stakeholders and forge national consensus around an e-transformation strategy and its implementation mechanism.

What should be the mandate, authorizing environment, and core capabilities of such institutions? How can countries minimize government failures and yet address market failures? What is required to strategize, implement policies, partner with the private sector, build alliances, and engage key stakeholders, without being captured by rent-seeking elements of the ICT industry or business community? How can these institutions prioritize, sequence, and coordinate investments, to respond to crises and opportunities and still be guided by long-term goals? All countries face these challenges.

Policy makers and e-leaders should address the following issues:

* What roles should government play in transforming a country into a networked society?
* What are the main institutional models for e-leadership institutions and what are their strengths and weaknesses? What are the emerging trends in developing these institutions?
* Why do countries need to develop e-leaders? What should be their roles and core competencies, and how to develop them?

DEFINE ROLES OF GOVERNMENT

The role of government in creating the networked society is evolving. Previous chaptersC have discussed the role of government as a major user of ICT in transforming governance and public services (Chapter 4); and as chief actor in the sectoral ecosystem being transformed (Chapter 5). Government is the ultimate policy setter and rule maker for digital policies and regulations that enable the development of networked societies (Chapter 7). Government is also expected to lead the development and implementation of policies and programs in support of digital inclusion and ICT-enabled poverty eradication, in partnership with civil society and private sector organizations. Government may also partner with the private sector in a variety of ways to pursue broadband infrastructural development, promoting supply, mobilizing demand, and securing universal access (Chapter 8).

Governments will inevitably invest heavily in public information systems and platforms, to run government operations. But they cannot afford to blindly invest in systems or outsource such services. Nor can they rely on private providers to define their transformational requirements and the consequent changes in managerial practices. Core competencies are needed within government to manage service level agreements, hold powerful global ICT service providers accountable, maintain well-contested markets for ICT services, and leverage new technologies for innovation and transformation.

Transformation programs within government and public services cannot proceed very far without a critical mass of staff with specialized skills in areas such as service-level agreements, public-private partnerships, change management and process reengineering, enterprise architecture, interoperability, data standards, data centers, cyber security, project management, ICT procurement, etc.—skills that must be embedded in contextual understanding of the business and services that the agency is in. Core technical competency and local expertise are also needed to alert policy makers on technological trends and cutting-edge practices and their implications for pubic policy and technology adoption. This is a fast changing technology. Paradigm shifts like mobile government, open source software, cloud computing, big data, and analytics are likely to have profound implications for ICT-enabled transformation.

REVIEW INSTITUTIONAL OPTIONS

Countries have adopted diverse governance models and institutional arrangements to lead the digital transformation process at the national level. Each governance model has its advantages and disadvantages and points to strategic tradeoffs that should be addressed early on in developing leadership and coordination capabilities for transforming governments and building an inclusive information society (Table 1).

Trends in e-leadership institutions. A review of e-leadership institutions in 40 countries provides discernible trends in the evolution of e-transformation institutions (Hanna, 2007b). First, there is a shift toward direct engagement of the president, prime minister, CEO or a powerful coordinating ministry such as finance or economy, by placing an e-transformation unit within close reach.

Table 1: Models of Governance and Coordination for Digital Transformation

Models	Countries	Advantages	Disadvantages
Shared Responsibility Model: Distributed sectoral responsibility with high level of policy coordination mechanism	Finland, Sweden, France, Germany	Integrates ICT agenda with relevant sectoral ministries with least disruption to current structures of government.	Functions well in relatively developed countries with strong traditions of political consensus, collaborative culture, and decentralized government. Does not provide for central push to overcome stovepipe mentality and build common infrastructures.
Core Ministry Model: Investment Coordination led by a cross-cutting ministry such as Finance, Treasury, Economy, Office of Management and Budget, or Planning Commission	Australia, Brazil, Canada (pre-2007), Chile, China, Israel, Japan, Rwanda, UK, USA	Has direct access to and controls funds required by other ministries in implementing e-government and other e-development programs. Helps integrate e-development with overall economic management agenda.	May lack necessary focus and technical knowledge/skills required for coordinating e-development and facilitating implementation.
Lead Ministry Model: Technical Coordination led by technical sectoral ministry – Communication and Information Technology, Science and Technology, or Industry	India, Jordan, Kenya, Pakistan, Romania, Ghana, Singapore, Thailand, Vietnam	Ensures that technical staff is available. Eases access to nongovernment stakeholders (firms, NGOs, academia).	Ministry may be too focused on technology, telecommunications, or industry, and disconnected from administrative reform processes.
Administrative and Technical Coordination Model: Led by Ministry of Public Administration, Services, Affairs, Interior, State or Administrative Reform for e-government, and by Ministry of ICT for connectivity and industry development	Bulgaria, Egypt, Mexico, South Africa, Slovenia	Facilitates integration of e-government with administrative simplification and reform, particularly when admin reform is driven by political commitment at high level.	May lack technology skills if exclusively led by administrative reform. Needs to share leadership with Ministry of ICT and perhaps others.
Designated e-Development Agency Model: Holistic Coordination led by autonomous dedicated ICT Agency	South Korea, Singapore, Ireland, Sri Lanka, Canada (2007)	Creates skilled, agile, business-like, high-performing entity that is relatively free of civil service constraints. Not dominated by the turf of sectoral ministries.	Vulnerable to changes in the authorizing environment and rivalry from the public sector.

Source: Adapted from Hanna, 2010a.

Second, countries have moved from ad hoc responses, informal processes, and temporary relationships to institutionalized structures to respond to the challenges of transformation. At the outset of the ICT revolution, governments convened special task forces, commissions, and panels to advise them. Typically these ad hoc bodies made their recommendations to ministers or heads of state.[28] The central message was to raise awareness of the role of ICT across government and society. Over time, these temporary bodies transformed into permanent institutions and formal coordination mechanisms.

Third, the locus of institutional leadership and coordination for e-government programs has been shifting from ICT ministries of central ICT agencies to ministries of public administration or interior, as in Korea. This reflects a shift in emphasis from technology management to institutional reforms, demonstrating the deepening transformational role of ICT. Similarly, digital transformation of specific sectors is increasingly led by corresponding ministries, working in collaboration with the central ICT agency or ministry.

Fourth, many countries are opting for an independent and strong national ICT agency that reports directly to the head of state or a powerful ministry such as Finance so as to address cross-cutting sectoral issues and lead the whole-of-government, whole-of-economy transformation. The agency focuses on policy and governance mechanisms such as whole-of-government enterprise architecture, and strategic investments. The shift to this model is driven by a growing recognition that e-transformation is a cross-sectoral, cross-hierarchical, cross-industry process, which requires political leadership, a holistic view of government, and ability to partner with nongovernment actors.

Fifth, as e-government programs mature, countries move beyond concerns about common information infrastructure, and toward organizing processes and services to fully integrate e-transformation into governance at all levels. In the process, the role of central

---

28   The number of nations who turned to such task forces is notable: Singapore in 1992, USA in 1993, followed by Japan, Korea, China, among others. See Wilson (2004).

agencies also changes from one of providing top-down and standard solutions to one of a catalyst for ICT-enabled innovation. The aim is to institutionalize process and service innovation, promote collaboration across boundaries, engage more stakeholders and disseminate best practices.

Finally, the content of e-transformation is changing over time, and e-institutions should evolve accordingly. As basic readiness and infrastructure are built, the emphasis shifts to a holistically supportive environment, bottom up participation, and other soft factors.

Draw on experience

E-leadership institutional development is one of the least understood areas of digital transformation. Consequently, building leadership capacity for digital transformation continues to be underlearned, and underfunded by governments and development agencies.

Strong centrally driven agenda and high-level political support are essential for e-transformation programs, but implementation will depend on the level of buy-in from the staff of the participating departments as well as the available management capacity at different levels of government. Resistance to change at the midlevel of government can be especially detrimental.

Many countries have been building public-private partnerships as a strategy for national e-transformation. National coordinating or advisory committees have been established, whose objective is to smooth out inherent tensions between ministerial mandates and the crosscutting of e-transformation interventions. Competition and cooperation are managed through well-designed committee structures that create bridges between the players who decide change, create change, and sustain change in the bureaucracy. Such structures take full advantage of ICT for service delivery and compensate for the traditional silo, ministry-based approach. They also secure the inputs of the private sector and civil society.

Effective interactions among e-leaders and between e-leadership institutions are essential to transformation. Social capital and enduring networks that link policy makers, civic leaders, academics, businessmen and the media are critical to the diffusion of ICT in society and the overall success of e-transformation, far beyond the soundness of any single leading agency. Social control of e-transformation should go beyond government. Successful countries have created a tight web of e-leaders and e-leadership institutions that cut across public, business, academia and civil society (Wilson 2004). Such a web can stimulate demand for sound digital policy, supply of necessary investments and skills, coordination of interdependent actions, and sharing of knowledge.

Trust, informal norms, and shared expectations are important in shaping this web of organizations. Leadership is essential to create conditions for trust and develop tight networks that cut across agencies and sectors. During periods of major structural change, the contribution of good leadership is invaluable. "Effective leaders provide the psychological and professional bridges between previous period of certainty and later periods of wider agreement."[29] Through their compelling visions, leaders provide meaning and direction in a chaotic world. They bridge boundaries, model risk taking, and show others the future.

Although there is no single solution, and those that work well in some countries may fail in others, there are common challenges that should be addressed by all aspirants of national transformation.

- Engaging key stakeholders to develop and implement a national ICT vision, strategy, and action plans.
- Developing a policy framework, laws, regulations and standards to enable transformations.
- Building high-level "executive" ICT function, responsible for leading the overall transformation process, and for coordinating multi-level and cross sectoral strategies and programs.

---

29 Wilson (2004), p. 93

- Developing effective division of labor and coordination of transformation programs across government agencies, creating an internal framework for collective decision-making on policy issues, and setting common ICT standards and best practices.
- Funding and creating special task forces for implementation of high priority e-transformation programs involving critical government departments.
- Creating mechanisms for monitoring and evaluation of major transformation investments across different government bodies and securing accountability.

In addition, policy makers should periodically review institutional arrangements, organizational models, and core competencies of their e-leadership institutions. This may be done every time a new national e-transformation strategy is adopted.

DEVELOP TRANSFORMATIONAL LEADERS

Countries need to bridge gaps that arise because of change management issues related to the new technologies. Technology leaders understand ICT but not the realities of governance, whereas officials and politicians may understand governance but not technology. A basic level of awareness is therefore needed for policy makers, legislators, opinion makers, and other public and business leaders.

Digital transformation brings massive changes in the work environment and requires staff redeployment, retraining and employment assistance to ease the process of adjustment. The more innovative are the uses of ICT, the more critical is the need for e-leadership. With the typically long implementation cycle of digital transformation, policy makers need to balance active promotion of ICT investments with absorptive capacity and retraining programs for managers and impacted workers.

One serious problem in many countries is the leadership's low understanding of the role of ICT in development. Increasing awareness among the business community is essential to enable the private sector play the role of catalyst and accelerator of innovation, and to press for government transformation. Government authorities and policy makers as e-leaders are the *porte-parole* of e-transformation. They should have true understanding of organizational and social impacts of ICT, and must develop the capacity to manage knowledge workers, learning organizations, local and global networks, intellectual assets, and open innovation systems. Lack of broad managerial understanding of the potential and prerequisites of the new technologies has been the key reason for failed ICT investments in both public and private organizations. But the problem is particularly acute in the public sector and in developing countries. On the demand side, executives tend to isolate and delegate ICT leadership to technologists and ICT managers, and are not aware of the critical role they must play to integrate ICT into their business or development strategies. One the supply side, e-leadership training tends to focus on narrow technological and technical issues, to the neglect of ICT-enabled strategic and institutional change and human resources issues.

A special cadre of e-leaders is the chief information officers (CIOs). In some governments, they are called chief innovation or transformation officers. In advanced economies, they are recognized as executives in their own right and treated on par with other business executives or CXOs. The roles, functions, and profiles of the CIO are becoming strategic and less technology-focused. In many developing countries CIOs and IT managers are engineers with technical knowledge but without management experience. They provide technology solutions but are isolated from the business they are in, and the external clients they must serve. In the public sector, they are placed further down in the decision-making hierarchy. Attracting ICT leaders to the public sector will require substantive change in both the profile and the compensation of this executive function.

CORE COMPETENCIES FOR E-LEADERS

As ***top executives and business strategists***, e-leaders should be able to visualize the destination of the information society, the results of an ICT-enabled development strategy and the possibilities opened up by ICT for their agencies and countries. They should be able to interact with and inspire other executives, stakeholders, and finally the organization or sector, to shape this ICT-enabled future. Their competencies in strategic thinking, strategic communications, and foresight should complement their domain knowledge of the business they are in. This should allow them to help lead the ICT road map for the organization at every level of operation. E-leaders shape and inform expectations for ICT-enabled and data-driven enterprise. They must be capable of creating frameworks and environments that bring ICT-enabled possibilities in line with business strategy, national aspirations and agency missions.

As ***change leaders***, e-leaders are chief innovation officers of new business processes and new forms of organizations. They are also the chief relationship officers who enable the creation of new networks and work teams within organizations, as well as new partnerships and supply chains across organizations. Working with other executives, they lead institutional change—their competencies help to evolve current hierarchies into agile, adaptive, networked, client-centered, and learning organizations. They lead process innovation, and client-centered service integration. They facilitate changes in skills, attitudes, and culture. They break silos, build partnerships, and engage process innovators, change agents, and organizational development practitioners. Leadership for change demands e-leaders to strike the appropriate balance through process and service innovation to build for the future.

As ***technology leaders,*** CIOs are the suppliers and custodians of ICT resources. This remains an essential role of e-leaders and the traditional domain for CIOs and chief technology officers (CTOs). Public service constraints often limit access to technical talent with knowledge of cutting-edge technologies, project management methodologies and new approaches to systems development such as rapid prototyping. Also in strong demand are skills to engage policy makers and business leaders in defining systems requirements and process transformation. Public sector CIOs manage networks of ICT service providers and engage in complex partnerships and contractual arrangements that demand current knowledge of the ICT industry and best practices. As e-leaders, they need competencies in outsourcing, portfolio management, project management, business development, and information resource management, along with a broad understanding of the technological environment—the trends, the new wave of innovations, and the ways and means to secure open standards and avoid the risks of technological lock-ins (Hanna 2010a).

Growing awareness of the use of data and information within organizations has led to a spate of new leadership titles, such as chief data officers and chief data scientists. The government of Singapore, for example, has appointed (August 2014) its first chief data scientist as it aspires to be a global analytics hub. The role of the chief data scientist and his supporting team, called the Data Sciences Group, is to drive the private and public sector's adoption of data analytics, including for cross-agency data. To increase the local talent pool, the government is recruiting consultants who hold domain knowledge besides their analytics experience, and has launched a MOOC specifically to develop the new cadre of data analytics leaders.

Developing Enabling
Policies and Regulations

———

THE DIGITAL TRANSFORMATION PROCESS REQUIRES that key public policy issues be examined for their impact on innovation, diffusion, and adoption of ICT. Equal attention should be given to formulating and implementing the policies themselves. A converged technology environment calls for coherent, technology-neutral policy and institutional frameworks. Political leadership and commitment to a long-term view are needed to secure effective regulation and sustainable transformation.

Policy makers, ICT leaders, and telecommunication regulators should address the following issues:

* Why regulate and how? What are the main competing policy frameworks that may guide the design of e-policies and enable e-transformation?
* What are the significant supply-side and demand-side ICT policy issues? How are recent technological changes likely to impact these issues?
* What major objectives should guide the formulation and implementation of Internet access and key IT policies?
* What are the implications of technology convergence for the development of effective regulatory institutions?

POLITICAL ECONOMY OF DIGITAL TRANSFORMATION POLICY

There are wider political economy challenges associated with public policy making and concomitant governance challenges in public institutions. Barriers to a transformational change are embedded in the political, constitutional, and institutional setup of a society, and should be explicitly addressed in any transformative policy reform:

* ***Government failure.*** Deliberate active or passive policy making is designed to divert resources or shape incentive structures of stakeholders to nonproductive or destructive activities. Ultimately such failure extracts economic value from the rest of society, to the benefit of a small elite (Acemoglue and Robinson 2013).

* ***Temporal asymmetry.*** In a short-term perspective, an annual GDP growth rate of 1–2 percent makes little difference from one year to another for the average citizen, and hence is not strong enough to shape the political agenda or electoral discourse. The dilemma of long-term growth is that contemporaries pay most of the costs (in terms of jobs, values, etc.) of a technology-led transformation, while the benefits are mostly enjoyed by future generations who are absent from the current political process. More formally, the challenge is caused by temporal asymmetry in the distribution of costs and benefits that shapes political agenda and electorate competition (Lipsey, Carlaw, and Bekar 2005).

* ***Regulatory failure.*** This occurs when public institutions are captured by private interest pressure groups or when agencies put their own interest above the public interest to protect the status quo.

* ***Private interest rent seeking.*** Not every private profit seeking is to the benefit of society (Hobsbawm 1969). Rent seeking leads to regulatory failure when policy makers fail to

distinguish between better public policy and better corporate deals.

- ❋ **Systemic failures.** Both federal and unitary states have to deal with dispersed layers of authority that are not coordinated and often in conflict with each other. For example, contradicting policy objectives are pursued resulting in systemic dysfunctionality and risks (Bianchi and Labory 2011).

- ❋ **Society's values.** Transformation requires nonconformist attitudes, increased openness toward new information, and tolerance toward the unfamiliar. The networked infrastructure that blends computing and communication is the largest construction project in human history (Cowhey and Aronson 2009). Getting public and ICT policy right or wrong has tremendous consequences for enabling transformational change that can deliver economically, culturally, and socially sustainable and desirable long term improvements in well being. The magnitude of socioeconomic benefits at stake is enormous.[30] So are the opportunity costs of narrow, biased, or extractive policy choices that could suffocate new initiatives, productive innovations, and investments in technologies underpinning the rise of the networked society.[31]

---

30 http://ictlogy.net/20080115-economic-benefits-of-icts/

31 The issue of rethinking policy and the opportunity cost of having the wrong public policy is summed up by Castell (1996): "If society does not determine technology, it can, mainly through the state, suffocate its development. Or alternatively, again mainly by state intervention, it can embark on an accelerated process of technological modernization able to change the fate of economy and social well-being in a few years."

POLICY FRAMEWORKS ENABLING TRANSFORMATION

Wealthy economies can be developed under a variety of policy and regulatory frameworks.[32] These economies meet a threshold of institutional quality that ensures political and economic stability, reasonable state capacity, enforcement of property rights and contracts, sufficient provision of public goods, and limits on government predation and corruption. Once the institutional threshold has been reached, the state can identify key industry issues, relevant regulatory approaches, important national objectives, and the right balance among stakeholders' interests to enhance long-term societal objectives.

Over the last thirty years, many countries have moved away from state-owned telecommunications monopolies, and adopted liberalization and deregulation to embrace a market-based regulatory approach that relies on competition policy. Historically, we have heard calls for less regulation, better regulation, more equitable regulation, smarter regulation, and now for more holistic regulation that focuses on the cumulative impact of regulation. Each of these calls serves as a reminder that technology moves faster than regulation and hence there is a continuous need for keeping regulatory frameworks aligned with technological, business, consumer, market, and societal realities.

---

32 The words policy and regulation are used interchangeably in this chapter with a broad meaning. Policy/regulation is the sustained and focused attempt to alter the behavior of others according to defined standards or purposes, with the intention of producing a broadly identified outcome or outcomes, which may involve mechanisms of standard-setting, information gathering and behavior modification. For further reading see Ogus (1994). Also, the relation between regulation and legislation is relevant to address here. If regulation is about altering behavior, then legislation is a subset of regulation. On the other hand, to the extent that regulation does not encompass tasks such as constitution making and dispute-resolution, the law is broader than regulation, in other words law and regulation intersect with one another but are not co-extensive. For further reading see Brownsword (2008), page 7.

A regulatory framework consists typically of three major elements as depicted in Figure 8. Its parts aim to answer the following three questions;

* Why regulate?—The policy rationale and legitimacy of interventions.
* With what ends in mind?—What regulatory objectives and desired outcomes are being pursued?
* How to regulate?—The matching of regulatory instruments to regulatory objectives and choosing of implementation strategies.

Figure 8: Key components of a regulatory framework

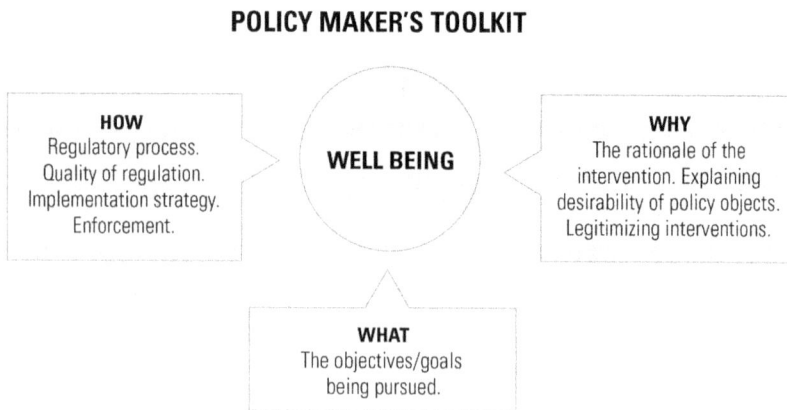

POLICY MAKER'S TOOLKIT

HOW	WELL BEING	WHY
Regulatory process. Quality of regulation. Implementation strategy. Enforcement.		The rationale of the intervention. Explaining desirability of policy objects. Legitimizing interventions.

WHAT
The objectives/goals being pursued.

Source: Ericsson, inspired by Weatherill (2007) and Prosser (2010)

A number of distinct regulatory approaches have emerged over time, each with a focus on specific regulatory goals and outcomes. Regulators do not typically pursue just one regulatory objective at any given point in time.

A ***market efficiency***-oriented regulatory approach is primarily based on competition policy focused on promotion of consumer welfare through maximization of market efficiency (allocative,[33] productive,[34] and dynamic[35]), and maximization of consumer choice and thus consumer sovereignty. It means the transfer from suppliers to consumers of qualitative improvements and cost reductions without restricting the market. Keeping markets open to new entry is a form of accountability for the exercise of economic power and hence maximization of consumer choice. However, opening up markets for more competition (market liberalization) can also restrict consumer choice, by ending cross-subsidies that have supported uneconomic services, customer segments or regions. Liberalization of the fixed telecom market, that started around 1990, constituted a move away from a public interest regulatory approach to a market efficiency regulatory approach. The introduction of multiple mobile spectrum licenses rather than relying on an exclusive license arrangement, and liberalization of the fixed telecom market, are two examples of how the market efficiency approach has been applied to ICT policy.

A *public interest*-oriented policy approach argues that there are serious limitations to a market efficiency approach as the latter treats all citizens equally and views all citizens solely in their capacity as consumers. Since we do not come to the market as equals, our market power as consumers is determined by our position in the existing distribution of wealth and information. This fact determines our ability to satisfy our preferences in a market. The public interest approach is a move away from market-based principles and may also imply a move away from

33 Allocative efficiency: when conditions of perfect competition prevail, and where goods and services are allocated between consumers according to the price they are prepared to pay, the price never rising above the marginal cost of production (sometimes also called static efficiency).

34 Productive efficiency: when as little of society's wealth is expended in the production of goods as necessary, so goods are produced at the lowest possible cost (the emphasis is on the internal management of a firm's resources).

35 Dynamic efficiency: refers to market conditions that appropriately balance short-run concerns—allocative static efficiency, with concerns in the long run—focusing on encouraging research and development (R&D). Through dynamic efficiency, an economy is able to further improve efficiency over time by making investments in R&D, education and innovation that act as forms of new market and demand discovery.

competition policy and a loss of market efficiency.[36] This move toward increased social solidarity is based on the idea that the state has a duty to ensure equal treatment of citizens irrespective of their economic resources. In ICT policy and regulation this approach is manifested by regulatory interventions that attempt to ensure equal access for all consumers (urban and rural) to vital services by requiring geographically averaged tariffs, rural subsidies, uniform standards of services across served areas, and requirements on a certain level of population service coverage.

Society also values aspects other than maximization of consumer welfare. Society building relies on the promotion of culture, social values and national identity. In countries such as Canada, most of Europe, and parts of Asia Pacific, such as Australia and New Zealand, regulation of broadcasting services is based on a public service media principle. Public service is typically associated with privileged access to scarce resources, limits to competition, and privileged access to state aid financing or public ownership. Support for a strong public service media continues to prevail in some jurisdictions while in others it is almost completely rejected on the claims of an inefficient monopoly and preference for a market-based solution.

A *rights-based* regulatory approach is not premised on a collective view but examines the individual's rights in a society or market. The regulatory rationale to protect some basic rights is globally less familiar than the competition or public interest-based rationale. The rights-based approach starts with the premise that all individuals have unconditional rights to certain levels of protection, and that some risks may be considered unacceptable whatever their benefits.[37] This approach to regulation can be encountered in various different policy domains, such as human rights, occupational health and safety, and environmental rights regulation. There are also private property rights that limit the regulators' rights to expropriate private assets, and procedural rights concern-

---

36 For more expanded discussion see Prosser (2005).
37 For further reading see Brownsword (2008) and Morgan (2007).

ing how public authorities, regulators, and courts operate (Sunstein 1990). ICT policy issues such as data privacy, the right to be forgotten, net neutrality, and open Internet concerns, all contain elements of a rights-based regulatory approach.

The ***networked governance*** approach is increasingly gaining attention, especially its applicability in an international context: the aim is to harmonize national and global policies. It is procedural and context specific (such as trade or Internet governance). It incorporates certain objectives, such as harmonization, coherence, etc. Networked governance combines state and nonstate actors and procedural means for resolving issues to overcome some of the limitations of governance based on territorial sovereignty. From a global perspective, the ITU's World Radio Conference, Inter-American Telecommunication Commission (CITEL), the Asia-Pacific Transport Working Group (APTWG), the European Conference of Postal and Telecommunications Administrations (CEPT), Internet Corporation for Assigned Names and Numbers (ICANN), and World Trade Organization (WTO) are examples of networked governance approaches. From a nation-state perspective, this approach to policy and regulation contains elements such as multi-stakeholder participation in consultations, forums that seek to learn and reach industry consensus, and increased attention to coregulation and voluntary industry codes of praxis.

A ***transformative*** policy is an emerging regulatory approach that is concerned with transformation of an industry or a society at large and more specifically focuses on the conduct of stakeholders in that process. It typically focuses on supply side policy issues, that is, the stimulation of innovations, R&D, and investments in new technologies and infrastructures, including public-private partnerships. There is also a growing focus on demand-side policy issues, that is, the adoption of new technologies and applications by various groups of end users—including consumers, small and medium enterprises, and public authorities. Increasingly, the aim is also to better align supply- and demand-side policies by removing inconsistencies between these policy areas thus increasing the socioeconomic impact by having a more coherent overall framework. Additionally, a transformative policy aims to enable more innovation: in new products and services; in the market place, consumer behavior and value; and in organizational skills, activities and capabilities. It emphasizes increasing productivity in an economy. In terms of national development strategy the emphasis is on competitiveness of nations or industries, Michael Porter's competitive advantage), and less on comparative advantage (David Ricardo, Adam Smith).

A transformative policy in the context of ICT constitutes a marriage of national broadband plans (typically supply-side oriented) and national digital economy reforms where the latter puts more focus on the adoption and use of new technologies. A transformative ICT policy aims to disseminate crucial ICT technologies and reshape all essential sectors of an economy.

The fundamental objectives of a transformational approach are to further a society's capacity for structural change in the most advantageous direction and the ability to preserve and increase the associated gains as the societal context changes. Some typical key policy goals are: competitivness, productivity, competence, knowledge-intensive and sustainable economic growth and digital inclusion.

KEY ICT-SPECIFIC PUBLIC POLICY ISSUES[38]

Some important ICT policy issues have significant impact on R&D investments (knowledge), value creation (innovation), roll out (diffusion), and use (adoption) of ICT. These policies determine the cumulative strength and sustainability of ICT in driving transformational change and in the distribution of socio-economic benefits. The topics, central to a transformative ICT policy agenda, impact the timing and willingness to invest in ICT, and the long-term supply of ICT-related capabilities. They also determine end users' (individuals, businesses, and public

---

38 Based on Ericsson (2014).

services) ability to benefit from ICT as they define the speed, scope, and intensity of opportunities and benefits available from ICT-led services.

Supply-side ICT policy issues

- ❖ *National broadband (BB) policies* aim to increase the roll out of BB infrastructure within a geography (region or a country) typically specifying an ambition in terms of expected BB service speeds, service roll out time plan, and sometimes adoption. They may also include public funding and cooperation mechanisms.
- ❖ *Network regulation* aims to address technical (standards), market (incumbent, new entrant) and consumer (protection, pricing) specific conditions with the aim to improve market efficiency, public interest (universal access) and increase protection of consumers (contract terms).
- ❖ *Spectrum management* aims to efficiently manage scarce resources and allocate new spectrum to highest value. Also includes global or regional coordination and harmonization of spectrum usage to decrease cost of technology by increasing economies of scale.

Demand-side ICT policy issues

- ❖ *Industrial Internet/Internet of things*—an umbrella term concerning emerging issue across a number of sectors currently experiencing accelerated rate of digitization such as, health, electricity, and energy. Increased use of ICT may result in changing relationships in existing value chains and in new business models, upsetting the status quo.
- ❖ *Media/content regulation* aims to regulate, increasingly in a multiplatform environment, obligations, roles, and responsibilities of media service and content providers while creating, aggregating, and making available audiovisual content.
- ❖ *Data protection* aims to regulate data subjects' rights and data controllers' and processers' obligations while collecting, processing,

using, and disseminating personal data. It also regulates transfer of data across national boundaries and roles and responsibilities in data processing value chains.

Horizontal policies impacting supply and demand side

* *Internet governance* concerns rules and principles for the operation and use of the Internet—the mandate, organization, and
  responsibilities of governing entities.
* *Trade policies* aim to regulate trade (financial, products, services,
  technologies, etc.) between countries and regions. Trade policies can facilitate liberalization resulting in more trade, economic and social integration, as well as transfer of technologies
  and innovations.
* *Intellectual Property Rights (IPR)*—an umbrella term including trade-
  marks, patents, and copyrights. The regime aims to protect private interest and increase incentives to invest in new knowledge
  creation and innovations on one side, and on the other, stimulate diffusion of new knowledge and innovation—for example,
  foster positive spillovers for greater societal benefit, thereby also
  limiting the private interest to appropriate some portion of the
  value attached to intellectual property investments.

Emerging policies impacting supply and demand side

* *Critical infrastructure and cyber security*—critical infrastructure
  refers to any vital infrastructure for the functioning of modern
  societies, such as electricity and ICT. The policy aim is to take ex-
  tra security measures—physical, logical, procedural, and redun-
  dancy—to assure continued availability beyond the demand and
  willingness to pay by the commercial market, as well as to cope
  with stressful environmental or other situations. Cybersecurity
  is a much broader term that includes considerations covered

by critical infrastructure, as well as additional considerations such as offensive and defensive measures to protect against and resist cyberattacks targeted ICT at any level: network, IT-infrastructure, software, device, and user.

- ❖ ***Big data and analytics*** refer to massive collection of data whose analysis drives innovation that creates new opportunities for society. Policies primarily touch upon data protection when they are applied at the individual level. When applied at the business level, they deal with issues of copyright, liability, and trade secrets. At the societal level they touch upon issues of open data, transparency and e-government initiatives.

INSTITUTIONAL QUEST FOR THE
EFFECTIVE REGULATOR

Digitization,[39] a product created by the ICT revolution, is the key driver of convergence, while the network, broadband, mobility, cloud, and smart-phones are the prime enablers of convergence. This technology driven process breaks up existing vertical service-technology specific value chains into a multitude of horizontal offerings and capabilities. Convergence changes markets by transforming traditional sectors, blurring historical market boundaries, and challenging the robustness of previously successful business strategies. Hence, convergence is a prime generator of new services, new capabilities, new ways of doing business, and new ways of orchestrating interactions in society.

From a policy perspective, convergence enables increased demand-side and supply-side substitution by lowering entry barriers and ultimately facilitating more consumer choice, lower prices, and increased competition and innovation. The outcome at stake in the hands of policy makers is how much a society can gain from the convergence process.

---

39 For more on digitalization and ICT technology advancements, see for example, Kressel (2007).

However, convergence puts a range of very different regulatory traditions and philosophies on a collision course:

* Telecommunications, concerned with operation of the physical network and access.
* Broadcasting, where licensing provides the basis for regulation on political and cultural criteria.
* The film industry, where control is exercised through classification, censorship, and copyright.
* Publishing, shaped by principles of a free press, libel, and copyright.
* The computing industry (including the Internet), historically left to develop largely unregulated, apart from general competition law.
* Protection of citizens' fundamental rights, such as privacy and free speech.

The vertical and sector-specific regulatory regimes that currently exist in most countries, comprising separate frameworks such as Internet, telecom, broadcast, content, and copyright, are increasingly inadequate for a converged environment and amplify the risk of dysfunctional market outcomes, suboptimal resource utilization, and an (un)intentional limiting of potential consumer surplus. A fragmented, vertical, sector-specific regulatory framework is increasingly problematic due to:

* ***Distortion of competition.*** Near-perfect substitute platforms (for example, terrestrial broadcast, satellite, telecom, cable, and Internet) should, in principle, be regulated the same way.
* ***Increased risk of overlapping policy remits created by convergence.*** A broad and holistic perspective that encompasses the reality of all converging value chains is necessary. By extension, policy makers need to rethink objectives, responsibility, governance, and forms of intervention.

- **_Weakening of regulatory effectiveness._** When alternative providers are less regulated, the lowest denominator prevails and becomes the norm in the long run. This situation creates an opportunity for regulatory arbitrage and distorts competitive and market-based business investment decisions.
- **_Regulatory flight._** There is a risk of companies moving to less regulated sectors and jurisdictions or being taken over by those outside the regulatory jurisdiction.

So how should policy makers respond? First, policy makers need to align converging sectors' overarching policy goals and desired outcomes and assure that remedies are applied equally across these sectors. This involves, among other things:

- establishing overarching long-term policy goals for innovation, competition, affordability, and availability, including standards for the lowest common denominator;
- ensuring a balance between investment protection and consumer interest, for example, balancing short-term gains against long-term economic viability across all sectors;
- increasing clarity of policy frameworks by examining justification for regulation (why regulate?) and outcomes (with what goals in mind?), aligning the objectives of economic policy with that of public interest, and ensuring that social (noneconomic) policy objectives are well targeted and have minimum distortion effects on competition and market efficiency.

Second, policy makers should adopt a technology-neutral framework. The starting point for creating a new regulatory instrument should be the service in question not the platform that delivers the service. Regulatory instruments and chosen implementation strategy should be service-specific rather than platform-specific.

Third, policy makers are faced with the challenge of whether established, vertical, sector-specific regulators should continue to constitute the most effective institutional setup to manage policies in a converged world. Once a converged policy framework has been formulated, the implementation, enforcement, and periodic overviews thereof are more effectively dealt with if the institutional setup is in line with market realities of the regulated sectors as well as the scope and mandate of regulatory frameworks put in place.

Effective and independent regulation remains essential to developing a dynamic infrastructure. Regulatory institutions need to be backed by research, training, and capability development. Ultimately, the success of new digital economy initiatives is preconditioned upon the presence of strong political leadership and a firm policy commitment that takes a long term view of the well-being of current and future citizens, competitiveness of industries, and social progress at large.

Developing the Communication Infrastructure

———

MOST ISSUES RELATED TO COMMUNICATION infrastructure are highly specialized and codified knowledge, and available in such sources as the World Bank/ITU's Telecommunications Handbook of 2011. This chapter primarily focuses on broadband communication infrastructure development and spectrum policies as they relate to the rest of the ICT ecosystem and inclusive digital transformation of society.

Policy makers may address the following issues as they develop their national broadband strategy and spectrum policy:

* Why develop a national broadband strategy? How do such strategies relate to the digital transformation ecosystem?
* What are the key steps for developing a national broadband plan?
* How to promote affordable supply of broadband?
* Why should countries pursue universal access and what user groups to prioritize?
* Why and how to mobilize demand for broadband?
* What policies may guide spectrum management in the era of mobile broadband?

DEVELOP BROADBAND STRATEGIES AND PLANS

To take full advantage of its benefits, policy makers should consider broadband in the context of the digital transformation ecosystem outlined in Chapter 2. This perspective comprises supply-side (network platform) and demand-side (such as e-government initiatives) considerations. To encourage diffusion of broadband-enabled innovations, policy makers should also take into account the absorptive (or transformational) capacity of various sectors such as education, health, finance, and small business. Unless all elements—supply, demand, and absorptive capacity—are synchronized, the impact of broadband on the economy as a whole will be constrained.

A first step in developing broadband plans is to assess existing supply and demand challenges. Next is to develop policies and strategies to address those challenges, setting measurable objectives to improve supply through infrastructure build-out, and promoting demand for services and applications. A clear sense of direction will encourage investment and provide a blueprint for long-term actions. The plan should promote efficiency and equity, and support national social and economic goals. Successful plans will include definitions of broadband, service goals, transmission capacity, service quality, and demand-side measures such as education and skills development.[40]

The government of the Republic of Korea was one of the early broadband leaders. It developed six plans since the mid-1980s that helped to shape broadband policy in the country. Korea shows that policy approaches can effectively move beyond network rollout and include user awareness, digital literacy, and technological capability development. It also highlights the possibilities for sector growth based on enabling policies and opportunity generation rather than on direct public investment.

Finland made it a legal right of all citizens to have 1 megabit per second (Mbit/s) access at affordable levels by 2010. By year-end 2015, 99 percent of all permanent residences are to have access, within 2 kilometers, to an optical fiber or cable network delivering 100 Mbit/s

---

40 For various definitions of broadband, see http://broadbandtoolkit.org/1

service. For Germany, the goal is 75 percent of households with high-speed broadband access at transmission rates of at least 50 Mbit/s by 2014. South Africa is working toward broadband penetration for at least 15 percent households by 2019. Sweden's goal was to have by 2010 near ubiquitous access to 2 Mbit/s service; by 2015 access to 100 Mbit/s connections for 40 percent of households, rising to 90 percent by 2020. The United States hopes to have by 2020, 100 million households with access to speeds of 100 Mbit/s and universal connections with actual speeds of at least 4 Mbit/s download and 1 Mbit/s upload.

Balance targets for access and speed. Countries differ in their approach to setting targets and goals. Some focus on improving access, while others set specific targets for data transfer speeds. One key issue for most countries is the proper mix of speed and access. Faster speeds are vital to taking advantage of new digital tools such as GIS mapping, telemedicine, distance learning, and video on demand. Questions have been raised in the United States about aiming for fiber-optic lines with 100 Mbps of speed when one-third of Americans still lack home broadband access. In balancing the competing goals of access and speed, priority may be given to high-speed networks for hospitals, schools and libraries, putting institutional anchors in communities.

Ensure stakeholder input. Planning for broadband must involve all relevant stakeholders, public and private. Governments should provide for a public consultation process for this purpose. Given the broad impact of broadband, these consultations are an important means of maximizing cooperation between the public and private sectors. Consistent with the holistic view of e-transformation, broadband development should be carried out in the context of national digital transformation strategies. This way, stakeholders' analysis, mobilization, and inputs for broadband plans and targets would be guided by national development priorities for transformation.

Provide a national focal point. Have a comprehensive national-level focus on promoting broadband use, experimenting with measures prior to national adoption, providing a clearinghouse for successful projects, and evaluating what works and what does not. To sustain this focal point, capacity-building programs must be developed for government officials.

Develop policies for both supply and demand. Experience in advanced countries shows that successful broadband diffusion requires addressing both supply- and demand-side issues. While supply-side policies focus on promoting network infrastructure for service delivery, demand-side policies aim to increase awareness and adoption of services.

PROMOTE THE SUPPLY OF BROADBAND

Promoting national build-out of broadband networks will likely require governments to pursue multiple strategies, depending on local circumstances. However, certain policy approaches may be globally applicable. The private sector is generally accepted as the primary driver of broadband development in most countries. Sufficient public funds may not be available for infrastructure investment, particularly in developing countries. Consequently, policy makers and regulators must consider how best to attract private sector involvement. A government will have to honestly evaluate the extent to which the country represents a profitable market for these investors, and identify strategies, policies, and regulations that can foster private sector initiatives. Many countries have taken this approach to facilitate and, where possible, accelerate, broadband roll out through regulatory measures rather than more direct forms of intervention.

In the developed countries and some developing ones, a majority of private investment may come from within the nation. In less endowed countries, attracting foreign private investment—through appropriate incentives, a clear regulatory and legal environment, and a good development plan—may be important components of a broadband strategy.

Governments have encouraged deployment of networks and improved competition by allowing, and occasionally, even requiring infrastructure sharing. The latter is mostly in areas where competing physical infrastructure was not economically viable (such as in rural or remote areas). By sharing network infrastructure, builders of networks can significantly reduce costs and make investing in them more commercially viable. This is particularly relevant for fiber-optic networks in rural areas, where revenues generated by such networks are low. Operators may have a commercial incentive to enter into these sharing arrangements. Operators may also be required to install multiple fibers in their cables, with the additional "dark" (unused) being held in reserve for future use by an existing operator or a new entrant. Thus installation, and the associated civil works, only need to be done once as opposed to multiple times with additional costs.

Infrastructure sharing allows telecom operators to develop common networks and share costs, thus reducing investment and lowering prices. Broadband fiber may be laid at the same time as new roads, railways, and pipelines, at low incremental cost. Fiber is cheap. It is digging that is expensive. Including broadband in land use planning may also promote build-out and reduce costs. For example, requiring all new housing developments to include broadband infrastructure, particularly fiber cables, alongside other utility requirements, can help lower long-term costs and avoid the higher costs of retrofitting.

Mobile broadband networks require high bandwidth backbones to support delivery. Upgrading backbone networks to fiber will support fast rising traffic. Policies to foster the development of national broadband backbone networks and to share infrastructure and spectrum are thus key to addressing a common bottleneck to mobile broadband diffusion.

With wireless networks, particularly in low-density areas, carriers can share cell towers and some backhaul facilities as a way of reducing network build-out costs and bringing competition to such areas more quickly. This concept has slowly been gaining acceptance in both developing and developed countries, as carriers seek to manage costs as they expand, or upgrade their services to support higher-speed broadband. However, this may sometimes face resistance from incumbents or dominant operators.

Where governments choose to finance their own broadband networks, they should avoid substituting for private investment or the normal market mechanisms. Effective broadband deployment requires a financing model in which government oversight and intervention are focused on funding only those initiatives that address actual or expected market failures and at driving early adoption of broadband services. Several other options exist, including government grants or subsidies to both private and public entities, and partnerships where private funding is matched by government.[41]

DEVELOP UNIVERSAL ACCESS TO BROADBAND

The idea of universal access to telecommunications now includes broadband services. The level of access provided is measured by the proportion of the population able to access the Internet and the locations from where access is achieved. Establishing fixed broadband connections for all households and businesses may not be a viable option in all areas due to the associated costs, lack of demand, and geographical constraints. At times, governments must assess the underlying goals of their universal access strategy and prioritize the most cost-effective means to achieve them.

In some national broadband strategies access for businesses, education, and government may be prioritized. This is often due to prohibitively high costs of Internet-enabled devices, subscription fees, and last mile connections. In addition, while many national broadband schemes may be subsidized or supported by governments, ultimately the aim is to create systems that support themselves by charging for use. Some countries thus prioritize access to anchor institutions such as libraries, schools, and government institutions—where broadband opens up access to large networks of information. Institutional access may also increase content available in certain languages.

---

41 For details of the main ways that government can support financing broadband development see World Bank's http://broadbandtoolkit.org/2.

Mobilize demand for broadband

In the most advanced countries broadband supply has increased substantially, and demand mobilization is taking central stage. In developing economies, affordability, sustainability, and the huge potential for transformation call for simultaneous attention to supply and demand. Consequently, demand facilitation is becoming an important part of broadband development policies.

So far, experiences in stimulating demand for broadband have been documented mainly from developed countries. These experiences must be adapted to the prevailing conditions in developing economies. With pent-up demand among users who previously had no access at all, the initial response is likely to be strong at the introduction of broadband, as it did in Kenya. As time passes, growth in demand is expected to slow down as users evolve from motivated early adopters to ones who do not necessarily understand what broadband has to offer and are more concerned with threats to privacy and data security. This is when government policies to stimulate demand may have the most impact. By educating users through digital literacy programs, governments can help to drive adoption to a broader user base. Such programs may become increasingly important as adoption rates rise, to avoid social and economic inequities associated with the digital divide.

Policy makers should conduct a diagnostic to determine the size and sources of the demand gap. Once this gap is quantified, it is necessary to understand the drivers of this market failure: affordability, digital literacy, or lack of relevant and attractive online content, applications, or services.[42]

Traditional measures to increase demand typically fall into three categories: awareness, affordability, and attractiveness. In order to drive broadband adoption and use, policies must address these three categories, especially targeting populations that are less likely to use broadband Internet services. Mechanisms to address awareness include: improving

---

42 For methodologies to measure the demand gap and conduct a diagnostic of structural factors affecting adoption, consult http://broadbandtoolkit.org/6.2.

digital literacy and encouraging the use of broadband in education and by SMEs; measures to increase affordability of both hardware and services; and measures to increase attractiveness. The last includes promotion of services, applications, local content development, and delivery of government services over the Internet (e-government).

More ambitious demand-side policy interventions, such as the Digital Agenda for Europe,[43] take a comprehensive view of stimulating adoption of ICT to improve long-term competitiveness of EU nations and the region as a whole. The EU Digital Agenda contains 101 actions including both supply- and demand-side actions, grouped in seven pillars, with the aim to enhance the EU economy and enable Europe's citizens and businesses to get the most out of digital technologies.

Another comprehensive approach taken by policy makers is to integrate a broader range of demand side policy actions on top of traditional supply side broadband interventions. Again the aim is to transform national economies and provide long-term sustainable socio-economic benefits. This approach is more common than is generally believed and not limited to developed economies alone. According to ITU[44] by the end of 2013, 134 countries had a national broadband policy in place. At least 60 percent or more of these plans had six additional action policy areas defined (see Figure 9) stretching beyond supply side broadband interventions (coverage, speed and timing).[45]

---

43 http://ec.europa.eu/digital-agenda/en/our-goals.

44 ITU World Telecommunication/ICT Regulatory Database and Broadband Commission.

45 For more examples of demand-side actions please refer to Broadband Commission report *Transformative Solutions for 2015 and Beyond*. http://www.broadbandcommission. org/documents/working-groups/bb-wg-taskforce-report.pdf.

Figure 9: Expanding Scope of National Broadband Plans

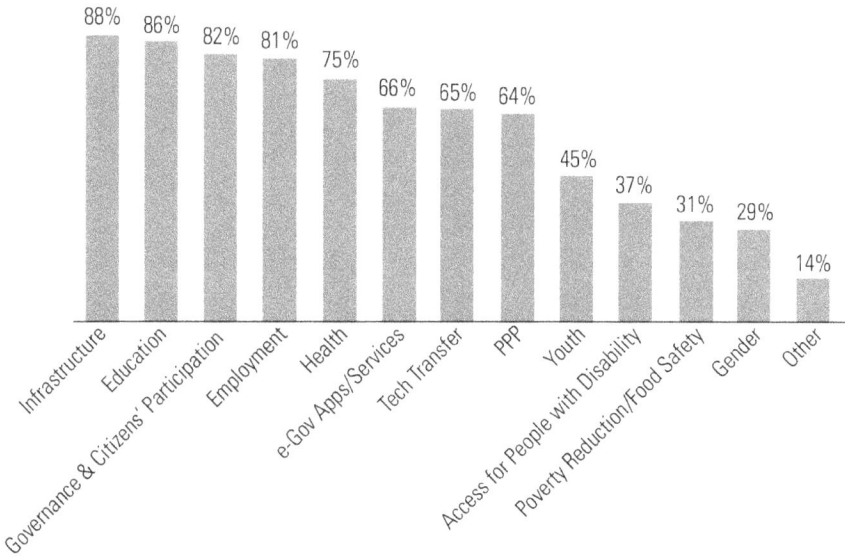

Source: ITU, 2013

MANAGE SPECTRUM FOR MOBILE BROADBAND DIFFUSION

Spectrum remains a scarce resource that requires effective management to ensure availability and quality (World Bank 2012). For rapid deployment of mobile broadband networks, operators need spectrum that is adapted to the most cost-efficient mobile broadband technologies. Blocks of spectrum must be sufficiently large to allow for cost-efficiency with multiple operators. Based on an assessment of spectrum needs, policy makers and regulators should release spectrum based on the following key enabling principles:

* economies of scale
* easy cross-border coordination and operation
* global roaming capabilities
* interoperability, choice, and affordability
* efficient use of spectrum
* maximizing the economic and societal benefits of spectrum usage.

It is also recommended that policy makers eliminate technological and services restrictions on spectrum. Eliminating restrictions, and making spectrum technology neutral, allow operators to select the most suitable technology to deploy on broadband services. Policy makers should also focus on expanding network coverage rather than on spectrum proceeds, as high upfront spectrum costs to operators may limit their ability to invest in coverage beyond the most affluent areas. To encourage coverage in underserved areas, Chile, Germany, and Sweden have added specific coverage obligations to mobile broadband spectrum licenses (World Bank 2012).

In 2014 there were about 7 billion mobile subscriptions globally; this includes all the 3GPP-based technologies: GSM/EDGE, WCDMA/HSPA and LTE. Within five years, the number of mobile subscriptions is expected to increase to about 9.3 billion, and at that time the number of LTE subscriptions will be of the order of 2.6 billion (Ericsson 2014). These astonishing numbers need to be kept in mind when 5G is being released for future consumer, business, and government users.

The continued and growing need for bandwidth will be propelled by the increasing number and density of people living in cities, using demanding audiovisual and social networking applications, as well as integration of vertical market sectors such as automotive, healthcare, education, and public protection and disaster relief. Further advanced applications are virtual and augmented realities, and new authentication and security systems. In addition, much of the demands for additional capacity are expected to be supported by the continuous improvements in capabilities of mobile devices with superhigh-definition video and imaging, and the notion of "presence" for people and things.

The current mobile technology families, GSM, CDMA, WCDMA, LTE, WiFi, Bluetooth and NFC, including their enhancements, will migrate to, or be part of, the 5G family of technologies, essentially complementing and overlapping coverage and capabilities between the existing generations and future 5G systems. Currently, research activities for 5G mobile broadband systems are focused on the increasing demand for ever-higher peak data rates, and the search for the ideal low latency configurations, while keeping end-to-end performance in mind at all times.[46]

New approaches are needed for the ITU and the WRC with the aim of responding to and securing the market developments mentioned above. Policy makers need to consider appropriate options, new procedures and structures. Bearing in mind that ITU is the only international body where global uses of spectrum can be fully discussed and reviewed, below are some suggested ways forward:

- Actual uses of spectrum need to be considered, rather than the strict subdivision of frequency band allocations of spectrum to services—reviewing if an allocation could be modified or shared.
- All current and planned uses of spectrum bands need to be reviewed and justified—not only the new entrants.
- Reconsider incumbent use if underused and/or sharing would be impracticable.
- Overlapping several allocations of frequency bands can adapt to needs for future very wide bandwidth.
- Map and mirror national broadband plans to the needs at international level while reviewing spectrum needs.
- Future spectrum work should be the responsibility of an expert group that has the interests of new entrants in mind.

---

46 METIS https://www.metis2020.com/

CHAPTER 9

Implementing, Monitoring, Evaluating, and Adapting

———

IMPORTANT LESSONS HAVE EMERGED FROM recent experiences of transformation toward a digital economy and information society. Although many of these lessons come from the rich northern countries, with longer experience in exploiting ICT, they are also relevant to emerging markets and less developed nations. Increasingly, developing countries are adding to this storehouse of experiences, as they appropriate new technologies, and in some cases even leapfrog and reinvent their uses, as with mobile technology applications, and especially mobile finance. Other complementary lessons come from long-standing (pre-Internet) yet relevant experiences in development and economic transformation (Hanna and Picciotto 2002). All these sources should guide, enrich, and enable new development policies and strategies, for countries at all levels of development.

This chapter sums up the lessons into ten fundamentals:

1) Commit to a holistic, long-term strategy.
2) Leverage stakeholder engagement and coalitions.
3) Tap synergies and scale.
4) Attend to soft infrastructure.
5) Pursue public-private partnerships.
6) Emphasize diffusion and inclusion.

7) Adopt strategic approaches to funding.
8) Balance strategic direction with local initiative.
9) Enable change, innovation, and learning.
10) Practice monitoring and evaluation.

1. COMMIT TO A HOLISTIC LONG-TERM STRATEGY

Transformation requires a commitment to the future. Pursuing the vision of a networked society or learning economy is not a quick technological fix or a one-time event. Countries such as Singapore have been pursuing this vision through successive five-year plans, each building on the foundation of the one before, setting higher and more inclusive goals, while delivering tangible results at each stage (Hanna and Knight 2011, 2012).

A long-term perspective facilitates the adoption of a holistic approach to national ICT strategies. It calls for anticipating, monitoring, and managing systemic interdependencies that guide changes over time. It enables planners to devise reforms and investments in a phased and sequential manner. It does not promise instant transformation. Rather, it helps stakeholders manage expectations, and set realistic markers in a long journey, so that at the end of the road transformation is successful and sustainable.

Transformation demands balancing near-term progress with a steady but not easily visible advance toward long-term goals. Countries with limited human and financial resources should focus and prioritize interventions for maximum transformative impact. Early learning, progress indicators, and demonstration effects of quick wins can help build confidence, commitment, and capacity for sustained policy reforms and institutional change. Pilots or small projects allow organizational learning at low cost and low risk. Funding a variety of grassroots initiatives can provide demonstration effects and tangible benefits and thus build a broad constituency for reform. But fast-track projects should be pursued within a holistic and sustainable e-transformation strategy.

Within e-government programs, some quick-win proposals are attractive because they expose civil servants and the public to new technologies and information-sharing practices, and thus mobilize demand and change the climate for participation and empowerment. An e-government strategy should also give due attention to foundational projects—ones that focus on establishing common infrastructure and architecture for the entire program. Foundational projects have long gestation periods, including lead time to build relationships with, and capabilities of, the owners of the new information systems, map and reengineer core business processes, and manage associated behavioral, organizational, and skill changes.

2. LEVERAGE STAKEHOLDER
ENGAGEMENT AND COALITIONS

Stakeholder engagement can be used to develop a holistic vision and a balanced approach to various elements of the transformation process. It can also provide new partnerships, promote innovative implementation strategies, mobilize local resources and communities, and ensure responsiveness to social needs and cultural diversity. Stakeholders, supported by dedicated and institutionalized leadership, build momentum and continuity for transformation. Transformational leaders engage stakeholders in framing the national ICT policy and generating broad-based consensus through consultative bodies.

A nationally shared vision of e-transformation helps to unify policies and programs and, at the same time, enables local initiatives and innovation. It engages local leadership in creating their own vision of e-transformation, and in linking and adapting national programs to local initiatives. In India, governors such as Babu Naidu, pursued their own local visions, which preceded and inspired the articulation of a national vision.

To avoid shallow and short-lived change, e-transformation should be based on an understanding of the political economy of the country as a whole and on building cross-sector coalitions and national consensus on fundamental reforms. Reforms can still be pursued incrementally, sequentially and dynamically, over time, building on success and evidence of impact, and in pace with the emerging national consensus. Occasionally, transformation initiatives are spurred by a national economic crisis, as in Finland in 1991, and Korea in 1997. Both countries are examples of concerted consensus building efforts that used institutional mechanisms in place to manage the transition from economic crises to knowledge economies. In the absence of a crisis, coalitions for e-transformation can be formed by raising awareness of existing global competition in an increasingly connected world. Chile is a good example, where a national e-transformation strategy emerged out of preparing the nation for an unpredictable future with increased global competition.

In some countries, coalitions favor a sector-focused approach to transformation. These can be harnessed and extended in support of the broad diffusion of ICT across sectors. User-centered coalitions (farmers, SMEs, women, students, etc.) are typically weak, as they are seldom organized. They can however be mobilized and merged into larger coalitions supporting cross-sector transformation. Effective networking and empowerment of such weak but potentially important stakeholders can be critical. Equally important is the mobilization of marginalized groups of ICT users. There is no better way to promote equity and social inclusion in the networked society.

Stakeholders should be engaged in setting realistic targets and managing expectations. A national e-transformation strategy should manage expectations about what is possible with ICT to accelerate development within likely resources. ICT is not a substitute for painful but necessary policy and institutional reforms. Rather, it is a catalyst. The strategy should be grounded in objective analysis of needs and constraints, systematic benchmarking, assessments of e-readiness and skills, and learning from past initiatives.

3. Tap synergies and scale

Digital transformation requires orchestrating the development of key elements over time to bring about sustainable impact and virtuous cycles. Integrated approaches are needed to exploit scale and network effects of ICT. Proceeding with ICT applications in isolation fails to assist countries in setting priorities, identifying cross-sectoral linkages, and sequencing interdependent investments. Fragmented initiatives also miss out on developing and utilizing scarce human, financial, and infrastructural resources.

Understanding the economies of scale on supply and demand is essential for a holistic approach to e-transformation (Shapiro and Varian 1999). Economies of scale on the supply side offer opportunities to share communication infrastructure, delivery channels, processes, and information systems development; provide access to ICT; consolidate data centers; create a critical mass of skilled human resources; and build capacity to adapt ICT products and services to the local context. The new information economy is also driven by demand-side economies of scale. The value of connecting to a network depends on the number of people already connected to it.[47] Technologies subject to strong network effects exhibit long lead times followed by explosive growth. As the installed base of users grows, the benefit for the users increases, and more users find adoption worthwhile. Once a critical mass of customers is reached, the market builds on itself with positive feedback and demonstration effects. Such adoption dynamics point to the importance of pooling demand, forming demand alliances, promoting open networks and standards, and investing in e-literacy to create critical mass and significant positive feedback as early as possible.

Unfortunately, holistic approaches do not come naturally to governments, politicians, policy makers or business actors. Digital transformation creates significant coordination challenges. Short-term political cycles and government budgetary practices reinforce the short-term and silo mentality,

---

47   This fundamental value proposition goes under many names: network effects, network externalities, positive feedback, and demand-side economies of scale.

and thus miss the synergies and interdependencies whose impact become evident only over the longer term. Leadership, policies, and institutions to bring about integration are missing, especially for new and crosscutting dimensions of development and competitiveness as e-transformation.

How can countries discover and manage these interdependencies? Here too the promising practices include developing leadership, shared vision, and consensus-generating institutions (as with Finland); engaging stakeholders, forming coalitions, promoting cross-sectoral collaboration; using budget, monitoring, evaluation, and other incentives to manage key interdependencies; having major users such as public agencies as anchors or drivers of e-transformation; and piloting integrated initiatives at the local level.

Leaders and e-leadership institutions are essential to integrating and orchestrating the various elements of e-transformation. Political, public and business leaders must engage stakeholders, forming partnerships, and leverage complementary assets to build the networked society. Some countries are more predisposed to collaboration than others; but most can learn to partner effectively.

Government budgetary practices can be a powerful tool for promoting integration and collaboration. In countries like Mexico, budget inflexibility and the lack of mechanisms for joint funding across organizations were considered major barriers to collaboration (OECD 2005). Some EU governments developed incentives such as collaboration as a measure for performance, and the provision of special funds for cross-agency projects.

Feedback, monitoring, and evaluation mechanisms are key tools to tap synergies, detect gaps, and strengthen linkages during implementation. To improve understanding of these linkages, it is necessary to focus on results and develop channels for timely feedback from stakeholders.

4. ATTEND TO SOFT INFRASTRUCTURE

Sustained transformation demands attention to enabling policies, leadership, and institutions—the soft infrastructure of digital transformation. Major political barriers may have to be overcome to create enabling policies for digital transformation. It takes local leadership, business initiative, and citizen activism to shape a shared vision, reform policies, and legacy systems, and build institutional foundations for a development paradigm shift. Effective leaders articulate an inclusive vision, linking interdependent actions to coproduce sustainable outcomes. Transformative leaders seek to understand stakeholders and engage them as enablers, partners, and implementers. Participatory national economic policy management seminars involving policy makers can play an important role in building national consensus and preparing transformative leaders, as in Finland (Hanna and Knight 2012).

Digital transformation calls for institutional arrangements that ensure the coherence of policies and investments to build common infrastructures, shared platforms, core capabilities and vibrant ICT ecosystems. For example, "open government" should be sequenced with the development of content, skills, and policies concerning regulation, data security, and privacy. Such an approach is important for developing countries where financial resources and skills are scarce, and prioritizing and sequencing are essential. Empowered existing or new entities can perform leadership, strategy, policy, and advisory functions, and implement, monitor, and evaluate programs on a continuous basis. Many countries are innovating and building the capacity of such institutions.[48]

Given the promise of new technologies and quick fixes, countries are tempted to bypass the efforts needed to develop the soft infrastructure.[49] But no off-the-shelf technical solution can substitute for institutional learning and in-house capacity to define visions and requirements, manage results, and hold vendors accountable for delivery. New waves of technologies continue to accelerate the pace of e-transfor-

---

48 For examples of such institutions and their roles in coordinating economy-wide e-development, see Hanna, 2007b.

49 The gap between ICT innovations and their diffusion and impact is significant. The rapid diffusion of mobile phones is an exception in view of dramatic decline in costs and low skill requirements for users. Yet, realizing the full potential of using mobiles for Internet access and development-oriented applications may take more time.

mation. However, taking full advantage of these technologies and integrating them on a large scale will require leadership and institutional competencies. New technologies open up new opportunities, but they also demand more soft infrastructure and transformative leaders, not less.

5. PURSUE PUBLIC-PRIVATE PARTNERSHIPS

Public-private partnerships (PPPs) present alternative ways to obtain goods, services, expertise and capacity building for the public sector.[50] These partnerships are contractual agreements between public agencies and private companies to supply infrastructure or services that traditionally were provided by governments. In a true PPP, the private sector partner not only stands to profit from a successful project, but also assumes some of the risks of failure. In contrast, under ordinary procurement contracts, the private sector vendor is likely to be paid whether the project is successful or not. Increasingly e-transformation projects have been the subject of PPP initiatives.[51]

The use of ICT in government presents opportunities to leverage private sector know-how and resources to accelerate public sector reforms. E-government initiatives in developing countries often suffer from lack of financial resources, low level of skills and capacity, and the absence of incentives to reward performance and innovation. Partnership with the private sector can help overcome many of these constraints, and at the same time increase opportunities for private sector development.

Partnerships are particularly critical to digital transformation of public services. Private sector partners experienced in e-commerce may have skills in online service delivery not readily available within the civil service.

---

50 PPPs were used mainly for physical infrastructure projects, such as ports and power plants. With rising demand for modern communications systems, PPPs have been developed around access to ICT resources. But PPP is not always easy to practice given the fast pace of technological change that can alter the balance of benefits among partners.

51 See IMF, "Public-Private Partnerships," March 2004.

Through appropriate business models and service agreements they may have strong incentives to mobilize demand for the online service, scale up rapidly, ensure high quality service, and minimize the costs of systems development, implementation, and operation. They may also have greater ability to raise funds necessary for planning and procurement.

As partners, NGOs can provide complementary resources such as local content and knowledge of target communities. Civil society organizations can also form coalitions to provide oversight and enforce reforms, as has been the case in the Philippines where e-procurement was introduced in the public sector to promote transparency and fight corruption.

With partnerships, e-government projects and services can be implemented more rapidly and at a reduced risk and cost to the government. At the same time, incentives provided to the private sector can deliver high quality services and scale up adoption. For example, the e-procurement system in Andhra Pradesh, India was based on PPP, where the private partner put up the capital costs, to be paid by the adopting users through transaction fees. This business model provided strong incentives for the private partners to promote adoption and system success.

PPPs are complex undertakings. They raise critical issues of implementation, legal frameworks, concordance with procurement rules and anti-corruption efforts, principles of selection of partners, and methods for assessing public costs and benefits in both the short and long term. So, where does one begin when it comes to PPPs in e-government, and what experiences are most relevant for specific needs?

To start with, here is a list of various forms of partnerships and their relative merits:

* **Design-build-finance-operate (DBFO):** The government specifies the services it wants and the private partner designs and builds a dedicated asset, finances its construction, and operates the asset, providing the public services required.

- **Build-own-operate (BOO):** The private partner builds and operates a facility or service without transferring ownership to the public sector.
- **Build-operate-transfer (BOT):** The private partner builds to specifications agreed upon with the public agency, and operates (but never owns) the facility for a specified time period, under a contract or franchise agreement with the agency. At the end of the period, the public partner, which always retains ownership, can assume operating responsibility, contract the operations to the original franchise holder, or award a new operating contract to a new private partner.
- **Build-own-operate and transfer (BOOT):** The private partner owns the project, invests resources, undertakes its development, owns and operates it for some time, and then transfers the assets to a public agency.

The key to the effectiveness of any public-private partnership lies in the strengths of each partner. Decisions on PPPs, outsourcing, and other contractual arrangements with the private sector have to be made carefully. Considerations include quality and quantity of government resources as compared to those in the private sector, the potential costs involved in outsourcing, and the timetable applicable to the project.

Although there is no set formula for crafting a successful partnership with the private sector, accumulating experience suggests[52] that the following elements should be taken into account (Hanna 2010b):

- **Political leadership.** Successful partnerships are formed only with top-level participation and commitment.
- **Planning.** Responsibilities of both parties to the partnership should be articulated in a contract, with clearly defined terms of risk allocation, change, dispute resolution, and termination.

---

52 See *National Council for Public-Private Partnerships (US), "Keys to Successful Public Private Partnership."* and InfoDev's e-gov toolkit, 2008, among others.

- **Legal framework.** The partnership should be built on a solid legal and policy foundation.
- **Compensation and mutual commitments.** The best partnerships involve clearly defined and shared burdens and rewards for both public and private participants. The PPP contract must explicitly state terms of minimum revenue, sources of revenue, user fees, fee caps, revenue caps, cost sharing, etc.
- **Public sector oversight.** Once a partnership has been established, on-going monitoring by the public sector assures its success. This is a clear weakness in many developing countries.
- **Consultation with stakeholders.** It is important to consult with all stakeholders in planning, implementing and overseeing any PPP.
- **Selecting the right partner.** Awarding contracts based on the best value, not just the lowest bidders, is critical.
- **Intellectual property rights.** Ownership must be clearly defined for assets in the form of products, technologies, and business models that may be created during project implementation.
- **Security and privacy.** Government must ensure that all sensitive data are protected against misuse. In PPPs, a private partner should not be able to use government's data for private purposes.
- **Exit strategy.** This goes beyond contract termination and into planning for government takeover, transitioning to a successor PPP or to government operation of facilities with full data protection and without service disruptions.

The success of PPPs in digital transformation depends on national e-readiness. Success factors include: access, quality and affordability of ICT infrastructure; government policy environment conducive to private sector participation; capabilities of the local ICT sector; potential for e-services adoption, including factors such as e-literacy and per capita income; and priority given to e-transformation on the public policy agenda. Assessing these factors should guide the pace and place of PPPs in national e-transformations.

Policy makers and aid agencies should keep in mind that PPPs are more difficult to implement for infrastructure that is subject to rapid technological change and uncertain benefits as is the case with ICT. Costs for ICT are falling rapidly, and it is difficult to foresee how benefits are to be best shared between private and public partners over the horizon. Innovative PPPs may also incorporate incentives for, and take account of innovation over the duration of the partnership.

6. Emphasize diffusion and inclusion

Most benefits of the ICT revolution are derived from applying ICT across the economy. Demand-side economies of scale also argue for pursuing diffusion and inclusion. Equally critical is the need to address the sociopolitical implications of the technological revolution since the distributional impacts are likely to be profound.

To ensure that digital transformation is both sustainable and equitable, policy makers must strive for early and wide diffusion of ICT, and systematically address the digital divide. Policy makers may start with providing affordable access and e-literacy programs. They may target public services, education, and employment opportunities that benefit the poor and those disadvantaged by the technological revolution. They may promote "frugal" innovation and affordable solutions cocreated with the poor and their social intermediaries. They may also consider ways to integrate ICT in propoor and safety net policies and programs to enhance their effectiveness, reach, and accountability to the beneficiaries. The search for inclusion must go beyond the ICT sector itself.

Innovation is critical to both diffusion and inclusion. Many countries and aid agencies are having troubles moving from successful pilots to scaling them up through diffusion that ensures sizable impact. Scaling or diffusing successfully innovative pilots helps reap network effects and economies of scale in supply and demand. But diffusion also demands innovation or "reinvention" as both technologies and organizations have to be modified to suit particular contexts. Innovation is typically needed when deploying ICT for poor communities, that is, when pursuing inclusion (Heeks 2013).

Acting on the interdependent elements of digital transformation can generate virtuous cycles in support of transformation and social inclusion. But these interdependencies also constitute barriers to digital inclusion, and if not addressed in time, could lead to vicious cycles of rising inequality and poverty entrapment. Case studies of developing economies like the Philippines and South Africa suggest the magnitude of the e-inclusion challenge (Hanna and Knight 2011 and 2012). Even in some of the most connected societies like Canada, the move from ICT access to broadly defined digital inclusion has been difficult, particularly for the rural and isolated communities. A national e-transformation strategy has to take an integrated and tailored approach to promote inclusion, fostering access to knowledge, e-services, ICT-empowered NGOs, and ICT-enabled employment.

Government must address barriers of competency, connectivity, and content along with the private sector and local organizations. For example, developing local content and applications can be costly, and requires upfront strategy, incentives, foundational support, training, and collaboration with knowledge sources at local and national levels. What policies and incentives enable low-cost development of content and local innovation of applications, and consequently encourage innovation sharing and scaling up? How can propoor applications leverage widely shared platforms such as mobiles?

Diffusion and inclusion require both integration and localization of e-transformation. At the national level, this would include creating enabling policies, and partnering with, and making resources available to local institutions. National programs should enable local institutions to use ICT as a tool for empowerment, social inclusion and delivery of basic services, and help build skills of participants to shape their own solutions.

The programs may also identify home grown low-cost solutions for knowledge sharing and scaling up to national levels. Advocacy campaigns and media exposure are necessary to change attitudes and practices.

Government may also engage the private sector and research institutions to customize existing products for the poor. Government may help aggregate the demand for new ICT products and services that are most relevant to the poor and seek ways to make markets work for them. For example, government may support and complement market forces by promoting low-cost access devices and open source and societal applications through cost sharing in product development and commercialization.

Blending and integrating various technologies may meet some of the needs of the poor. Older technologies such as radio and television may be blended with Internet and mobile telephony for some simple but relevant applications for poor communities. Community radio still holds much promise, and can be used in combination with Internet to deliver health and agricultural extension services. At times, however, the latest technologies are the most user friendly and least demanding in terms of technical or literacy capabilities, as has been the case with mobile phones.

7. ADOPT STRATEGIC APPROACHES TO FUNDING

A variety of financing mechanisms, both strategic and flexible in approach, are needed to develop various elements of the e-transformation process. Some of the elements require upfront and sizeable investments as in telecommunications infrastructure. Others require long-term commitments, such as human resources development. Some call for coordination among government agencies, as in e-government, while others demand venturing, innovation, and experimentation before scaling up as in community information centers and local content development for education and rural areas. Certain aspects of e-transformation are more attractive for the private sector, as in telecommunications, while others require diverse financing and cost-sharing partnerships as in shared access centers (telecenters).

By removing regulatory obstacles to competition, governments harness private sector and FDI to help meet public policy objectives of developing broadband and extending access. Market-based approaches have proven effective for leveraging the financial resources and operational expertise of the private sector to meet universal access goals. However, in many rural and remote areas, market forces are not adequate to meet economic and social goals, and public financing may be used to provide competitive subsidies or form PPPs (Chapter 8).

Developing countries are vulnerable to worldwide economic downturns and financial cycles. However, some transformation programs require upfront, steady and predictable funding over the medium term. Studies of e-government programs in OECD countries suggest that a number of budgetary practices work against effective planning and management of these programs: short time horizon (single-year expenditure horizon) for projects that require long term commitments; agency by agency budgeting that prevents shared funding for common systems and shared infrastructure; lack of incentives to share benefits among agencies that could eliminate redundant systems; and difficulty of measuring costs and benefits for e-government projects compared to other traditional infrastructure investments (OECD 2003). Government budgetary practices tend to be inflexible—not amenable to capturing the synergies among investments or crosscutting dimensions of e-transformation.

A common challenge to funding e-government programs, in particular the shared infrastructure required for a whole-of-government approach, is the agency-by-agency appropriation of public expenditure. For example, in early 2000, the US Office of Management and Budget secured significant funding for major crossagency projects, to develop the necessary horizontal building blocks for integrated government, back office modernization, and information infrastructure consolidation. The majority of ICT funding in US government remained under the line agencies, following the traditional approach of appropriation by Congress, and in line with vertical accountability. Despite the break-through of authorizing a central fund for key interagency projects, much of the authorized resources were not requested by the lead implementing agencies, and thus remained unutilized. Clearly, the budgetary incentives were not strong enough and the political economy for e-government was not supportive for crossagency collaboration.

Box 2: Korea's Flexible Financing for E-development Initiatives

The promotion of ICT adoption in government and overall economy requires large-scale and long-term investments and cooperation across government agencies. It is difficult to carry out these projects within the general budget of Korea. The Informatization Promotion Fund (IPF) was established in 1996 as a special vehicle to overcome the budgetary rigidities and promote e-government projects across agencies by providing a flexible central financing mechanism for transformation initiatives.

The goals of the IPF are to roll out broadband networks, promote e-government projects, educate workers and support R&D and standardization in ICT in a holistic approach to government and economic transformation. The fund, based on government budgetary and private sector contributions, promotes the use of profits from ICT fields to be rechanneled into the ICT sector. From 1993 to 2002, the IPF reached US$ 7.8 billion, with 40% coming from the government budget. A total of US$ 5.3 billion was invested in between 1994 and 2003. The Ministry of Information and Communications (MIC) is the overall manager of the fund, along with the Institute of Information Technology Assessment (specific project management), and the Fund Management Council (evaluation). The chair of the council is the vice minister of the MIC, and its members are members and directors general of related ministries.

The IPF played a key role in holistic and flexible promotion of e-transformation (informatization) policy to create demand for ICT-enabled transformation, while promoting supply through a competitive ICT industry.

Adapted from Suh and Chen, 2007. p 92.

Financing e-transformation is particularly challenging for developing countries where time horizons are often short due to political and economic uncertainties. But e-transformation is a continuous process of policy development, investment planning, innovation, learning, and change management. This process must fit in with and respond to a dynamic strategy that supports evolving national goals and creates sustained institutional reforms and service improvements. The challenge is to build effective governance and institutional frameworks for ICT-enabled transformation, and make the new competencies integral to the country's human and organizational resources. Rather than seeking agreements on rigid investment plans, the focus may shift to reforming and institutionalizing budgetary and financing frameworks to adopt a medium-term perspective and integrate other sources of funding, from business, NGOs, and aid agencies.

Republic of Korea provides an example of strategic yet flexible funding for digital transformation (Box 2).

8. BALANCE STRATEGIC DIRECTION
WITH LOCAL INITIATIVE

We are entering a new world we cannot fully predict, much like the transition from the preelectric world to that of electric utility and ubiquitous grid—those who witnessed the beginning of that transition could not anticipate how electricity would transform their lives and economies (Carr 2008). E-transformation is a complex phenomenon in a fast-changing global technological environment. It is still in flux, with no easy answers or codified strategies to scale. ICT may be used to transform societies and economies in ways that cannot be fully foretold at present.

The versatility of ICT has to be matched by a willingness to understand the social and institutional contexts within which the technology is applied. E-transformation involves joint investments in complementary factors. It deals with intangibles such as knowledge, innovation, learning, software, and cultural and organizational change. It is also linked to issues of communications, language, identity, control, and empowerment. Much of these intangibles are context-specific and subject to local understanding and decisions. E-transformation cannot be under the exclusive power of a central agency; neither can it be bought as a blueprint plan or turnkey solution.

Localization of knowledge and content is essential to digital transformation. Technology-driven visions of downloading global knowledge are misleading (Stiglitz 1999). The vast variety of human societies requires localization of knowledge, especially tacit knowledge. Each society should take an active role in this learning process and local content creation. The growth of community access to the Internet, community networks, digital literacy, and social-media tools help locally driven social production, adaptation, and application of information and knowledge.

Countries therefore need to develop capabilities to acquire, adapt, maintain, customize and reinvent existing "ICT solutions" to meet their specific requirements under diverse local conditions. Experience shows that dirigist central planning fails in pluralistic environments. Not only is local initiative essential to effective appropriation and integration of ICT into development activities, but also ICT can be a powerful enabler of decentralized and grassroots development across sectors (Hanna 2009).

So, what should be the role of national strategies? Experience shows that a national transformation strategy, backed by international best practices, can facilitate consensus, engender ownership, promote shared understanding, induce policy reforms, set strategic directions that reflect national priorities, and mobilize complementary resources. It can provide an objective and transparent process for prioritizing transformation activities across the economy.[53]

Yet, formulating a national strategy through a top-down process has its risks and limitations. Rather than emphasizing an iterative and adaptive process, top-down strategic exercises risk rarifying the final planning document and glossing over the original assumptions, thus undermining continued learning, strategic thinking, local initiative, and grassroots innovation. These risks are magnified when aid agencies working in poor countries hire unfamiliar international consultants to carry out pro forma strategic planning exercises and end up buying standard recipes, or national ICT strategy documents that are not grounded in local diagnosis or linked to local initiatives and aspirations.[54]

---

53 Many prioritization schemes, designed for use in developed countries, involve high levels of quantification and sophistication. Care should be taken to use methodologies that are consistent with local conditions, including capabilities and the availability of demand data.

54 Similar arguments are made against adopting a standard recipe for growth strategies and institutions in Rodrik (2007).

Orchestrating top-down and bottom-up initiatives can create powerful e-transformation dynamics. Top-down directions will set the overall vision, create awareness, build coalitions, establish e-leadership institutions, invest in shared infrastructures and capabilities, and evaluate progress toward development outcomes. Grassroots innovation funds may be used to provide matching grants in support of bottom-up proposals for ICT-enabled community innovations, digital local content, local capacity building, local partnerships, e-literacy, digital inclusion, and last-mile connectivity initiatives. A combined bottom-up and top-down transformation process should develop mechanisms to support pilots and rapid-results projects, and to scale up successful pilots into a critical mass of national initiatives. This combination will then lead to the adoption of deeper institutional change, long-term reform agenda, institutionalized monitoring and evaluation, and fast learning cycles.

Striking the right balance depends on political and administrative culture. Countries with more plural and decentralized traditions, and active and informed civil society, such as Canada and Finland, are likely to adopt more flexible national e-transformation programs informed and influenced by local initiatives, put resources and capabilities at the local level, and support local experimentation and innovation. In other countries, such as Korea and Singapore, the initial push for e-transformation has been top-down with clearly defined goals and foundational investments, and only later came the search for bottom-up innovation and deep transformation. For example, Singapore has lately created an innovation fund to support bottom-up changes within government. As countries advance toward more connected governments and networked societies, e-transformation programs have to become more flexible, pluralistic, community-based, and locally driven, enabled by selective and strategic central investments.

9. ENABLE CHANGE, INNOVATION, AND LEARNING

Why is change management so critical to successful implementation of e-government programs? How can governments move from a culture of compliance and risk aversion, to one where innovation is celebrated and change is deemed necessary for superior performance? Can public agencies practice reengineering and "imagineering" of their processes and services? Why and how should public policy promote sociotechnical innovation and learning throughout the e-transformation economy and society?

There is no standard change management strategy, since there are many factors that facilitate or inhibit change: political economy, leadership, culture and skills of the civil service, local business, influence and support of other stakeholders, the stakes involved, and time frame for implementation. The changes required for transformation range from technology and process to work habits, skills and incentives of employees; organizational structure and decision making styles; legal and regulatory policy changes; and, at the broadest level, sociopolitical changes involving reforms and empowerment issues.

The biggest challenge for transformational change in government lies in getting organizational buy-in and dealing with attendant change management issues. Over and above a clear political intention, there must be a serious assessment of political and administrative mechanisms to ensure that they have the depth and maturity to manage change. Political and civil service leadership must also have the capacity to cope with hard choices and tradeoffs, such as skill upgrading and staff redeployment. The sociotechnical change accompanying sector transformation demands retraining of existing staff, hiring high-quality new staff, updating managerial skills, managing resistance to change, and sharing data with other agencies. It also requires incentives for innovation and initiative, partnership with the private sector, and with unions and staff associations. Managerial skills are often more critical than technical skills in the context of change, as there are more managerial and organizational innovations required than technological.

E-transformation is an adaptive learning process. Many details of e-transformation strategy will emerge from a learning process during strategy design and implementation. As distinct from a blueprint approach, this approach is biased toward action and learning. It is flexible, evolutionary, participatory, and results-oriented. It builds on local learning and adaptation by combining top-down strategic approaches with vibrant and diverse bottom-up local initiatives (Hanna and Picciotto 2002). There are many ways to do this through online, real time methods, including social networks and monitoring software. But staff must be trained and allocated to this task.

Institutional mechanisms for developing and implementing transformation strategies should be worked out with the stakeholders, and with oversight and political commitment at the highest levels. E-transformation programs rely on results-oriented monitoring and evaluation for timely adjustment and adaptive planning. They require relentless pursuit of citizen feedback. The programs build capabilities and access to resources so that the community participates, appropriates, and adapts ICT at the local level. They build the ecology of collaboration.

Innovation funds (innovation challenges) may be created to provide small grants to finance pilots and bottom-up innovations that will demonstrate microreforms in government and in sectors. Change agents at the lower rungs of government are often aware of opportunities to improve client services, but are stifled by the concentration of resources and power at the top. Yet, institutional change and macro reforms often spread through microlevel changes that, when strategically managed, will aggregate into large-scale transformation.

A flexible and decentralized framework, which takes into account diverse conditions and opportunities, empowers change agents at all levels. The role of top leaders is to create an enabling environment with a budget process resembling venture capital funds to support micro financing of innovations, and knowledge sharing mechanisms and communities of practice to disseminate innovations. Brazil has developed an observatory of ICT practices in government to capture and disseminate ICT-enabled innovations (Hanna and Knight 2011). In the United States, the federal CIO council plays a similar role. Despite such examples, many governments tend to "reinvent the wheel" by investing repeatedly and separately in software applications and process reengineering designs for otherwise similar services and functions. Even within Brazil, many local governments have proceeded with developing their own ICT applications and e-government portals for the same basic functions. There are some islands of excellence, to be sure, but their practices and innovations are seldom shared. Lacking independent evaluation, pilot e-government innovations are often declared a success before ensuring sustainability.

Countries are learning more about tools that stimulate innovation and learning equally in government agencies, enterprises, and grassroots organizations. They include creating innovation marketplaces, providing competitive grants for innovation, engaging external partners and users, creating customer or citizen feedback loops, and involving stakeholders with diverse perspectives. Unfortunately public agencies often approach innovation as a "one-off" change instead of steps that systematize the process and develop a culture of innovation. To do so, a central task for transforming government and society would be learning at all levels.[55] Countries may invite leading ICT multinationals, specialists in the diaspora, and international talent to participate in their learning process, share experience, benchmark themselves against the best, and build forums for sharing and blending external and local

---

55 A key message from the fast transforming countries, this is particularly true for a new sector attempting to master a general-purpose technology such as ICT. Singapore and Finland created a high-speed learning environment and made their economies test-beds for ICT innovation.

learning,[56] while staying grounded in local realities and linked to the needs of the community.

OGD too can spur innovation. Demands for accountability and good governance lead to improvements in public services. Such demands can be captured through citizen feedback on services and devising the right metrics to measure results. Open data can also promote public-private partnerships. Grassroots organizations can play a key role in mobilizing political capital and social innovators to demand community-defined results, push for creative solutions, and counter risk aversion. Small-scale experimentation can be used to gradually shift the culture of government toward openness and collaboration. Direct engagement with citizens or social intermediaries is a new experience for civil servants the world over. This requires incentive to listen to citizens and to increase understanding of client needs and behavior. Fortunately, new collaborative technologies are making the process easier.[57]

10. PRACTICE MONITORING AND EVALUATION

Monitoring and evaluation (M&E) are essential to sustainable transformation. Early design of M&E systems can guide the overall design of the e-transformation strategy. Systematic capture and sharing of innovation and implementation experience can also reduce learning costs and augment integration of learning into practice. M&E should apply throughout the duration of a transformation program. It should measure progress, support midcourse corrections, and guide resource allocation

---

56 In seeking FDI, Singapore was selective and targeted in its incentives and recruitment, emphasizing quality of investment, tapping global knowledge, attracting innovative and leading ICT firms and their research and learning arms, maximizing spillover effects, and building an expanding pool of highly skilled human resources.

57 Singapore, with a tradition of top-down strategy, has recently reoriented its transformation efforts to rely on collaborative government and collaborative innovation. Government still steers the fundamentals such as developing an enabling policy environment, coinvesting in broadband, and promoting partnerships for innovation and technological capabilities. But it is learning to listen to clients, to seek partners, and to collaborate with all segments of society.

decisions. Too often governments do not consider evaluation metrics until after program launch or even completion. Few governments in developing countries invest in measuring the impact of e-government. Lack of appropriate M&E will inhibit the learning process as well as the identification of best practices for continued adaptation.

Development practitioners in general and ICT professionals in particular have mostly focused on the physical and the measurable: investment in ICT hardware and software, telecom penetration, connectivity measures and indices, etc. Without meaningful and comprehensive indicators of ICT usage and impact, it is impossible to have a complete picture of the role of ICT in transformation, or learn about the intangibles that are much harder to measure, but no less important. These intangible assets are the accumulation of knowledge embedded in people, institutions, processes, and their interactions. They are the important outcomes of experimentation, learning by doing, and institutionalized evaluation.

M&E should occur at several levels. On the national level in the United States, for example, the OMB tracks agency-by-agency progress toward government-wide e-government goals. Program level evaluations should be done throughout a program, so that findings can be acted upon and deficiencies corrected. Monitoring and evaluation should refer back to goals and metrics laid down at the planning phase. Therefore, it is important to invest time and resources in defining key performance indicators (KPIs) and other metrics at beginning of the program and to create a coherent plan for monitoring and evaluation. Institutionalizing evaluation can help set priorities among investment proposals within and between public agencies, as it leads to better understanding of factors influencing costs, benefits, and reach to beneficiaries.

E-government evaluation methods and practices raise several challenges. Evaluation narrowly focused on ICT investments can discourage collaboration with other programs of public sector reform. Evaluation of cross-agency projects often fails to take into account costs borne by the funding agency and benefits shared across agencies. Another challenge is to create incentives for longer-term transformation programs. M&E tends to reinforce the short-term perspectives. Yet, OECD studies suggest that transformational projects for e-government produce more than three times the benefits for government and users than individual projects to deliver e-services (OECD 2005, 111).

Given the fast pace of technological change, traditional M&E systems are often inadequate for the task of adapting and learning from implementing e-transformation. Agile learning systems are required. Such learning systems should address the needs of all stakeholders as well as intended beneficiaries. Given the lag in producing development outcomes, evaluation must be participatory and frequent. Rapid participatory assessment methodologies can be designed to learn from stakeholders and beneficiaries at the local level (Hanna and Picciotto 2002).

A common pitfall is to overdesign M&E systems to generate massive and expensive data collections and surveys that remain unutilized. A related pitfall is to overemphasize detailed targeting and tracking so as to micromanage at the expense of shared visions. A sophisticated M&E system without a shared vision of the future is unlikely to motivate or sustain deep change.

International aid practices tend to orient M&E to external accountability and research, at the expense of cultivating capabilities, initiatives, adaptation, and learning at the local level. E-transformation strategies often have little precedent to go by, making it difficult for stakeholders to agree on indicators or to grasp the scale of required inputs and resources. A premature introduction of overly complex M&E systems can thus be costly as it will divert resources away from more practical and timely learning that can come from simple, homegrown, locally owned solutions. It can also delay the design and introduction of practical M&E at early stages of the implementation of e-transformation. Simple and transparent M&E systems are also more comprehensible and useable by local stakeholders and grassroots organizations as well as external partners.

Alternative approaches should leverage the capacity of local M&E agencies and networks, including those of ICT-using sectors. They may also introduce ICT-related indicators into ongoing household and enterprise surveys and others being conducted by the national statistical office. M&E instruments for e-strategies should be made as compatible as possible with existing M&E instruments for the national development strategy, so as to reinforce linkages with national development objectives.

One strategic choice in institutionalizing M&E is whether to embed this capacity into the implementation structures of digital transformation programs, or locate it at the highest policy levels, independent of the implementing agencies. A common pitfall is making an either/or choice. M&E capabilities are needed at many levels. Embedding M&E into implementation structures leverages existing capacity, access to data, ownership, and learning. Having M&E capacity at the highest independent level is important to secure oversight and accountability, authority and influence to make course corrections, and perhaps promote more focus on development impact. A balance may be established between self-evaluation (internal to implementing agencies) and independent (external) evaluation systems.

M&E indicators should reflect the sequencing of strategy objectives, starting from policy objectives such as diversifying the economy and improving education, and moving to specific outcomes of e-transformation initiatives and actions. The World Bank has developed a toolkit to integrate M&E indicators into a logical framework (Adamali et al. 2005). At the first level of logframe are the development impacts of policy goals of the country. At the second level, impact indicators should determine the outcome indicators for the strategic priorities of transformation. The third level considers output indicators of key initiatives. The fourth level is concerned with deliverables of key actions. The base level considers inputs and resources required to implement e-transformation. Such conceptual frameworks can be helpful in systematizing and improving M&E practices. But any advance will be conditional on country commitment to adapt these frameworks to their local situations, clarify causal links within specific local contexts, and provide concrete examples of using such frameworks for strategic choice and learning.

A FINAL WORD

At the core of effective and sustained digital transformation is the institutional and societal mastery of processes that cause deep sociotechnical change.

Transformational leadership envisions and communicates a desirable future that can facilitate cooperation, mobilize resources, and build consensus on actions for the long term. An energizing vision can also facilitate flexibility and innovation while maintaining consistency in strategic intent. Commitment to experimentation and learning helps maintain policy flexibility and avoids ideological lock-ins, while securing sustained commitment to transformation. Digital inclusion can augment demand and maximize impact while enhancing social cohesion and human resources development. Inclusion is achieved through national consensus, and local innovation, experimentation and learning. In turn, widespread diffusion of ICT and its tangible benefits lends support to visionary leaders, pioneering institutions, and the emerging social consensus for e-transformation.

Most countries are still at early stages of their e-transformation journey, and have much to learn from within, from each other, and particularly from the pioneers. While the journey is going to be demanding and full of uncertainties and discoveries, it is necessary to harness the ongoing technological revolution and realize its potential for aspiring nations. Some technologies may be leapfrogged, but mastery of the ICT-enabled transformation process has to be learned at the individual, institutional, and societal levels. Mastering this process will likely be the defining core competency of the twenty-first century.

REFERENCES AND SOURCES

Abramson, Mark, Breul, Jonathan, and Kamensky, John. *Six Trends Transforming Government*. Washington, DC: IBM Center for the Business of Government. 2006.

Accenture. *Build It and They Will Come? The Accenture Digital Citizen Pulse Survey and the Future of Government Operations*. Washington, DC: Accenture. 2012. http://www.accenture.com/us-en/Pages/insight-digital-citizen-pulse-survey-summary.aspx

Acemoglue, D., and Robinson, J. *The Origins of Power, Prosperity and Poverty*. New York: Crown Publishers. 2012.

Atkinson, Robert, and Castro, Daniel. *Digital Quality of Life: Understanding the Personal and Social Benefits of the Information Technology Revolution*. Washington,: the Information Technology and Innovation Foundation. 2008.

Australian Government Information Management Office (AGIMO). *Interacting with Government: Australians' use and satisfaction with e-government services*. ACT: AGIMO. 2011 http://www.finance.gov.au/publications/interacting-with-government-2011/index.html

Badshah, A., Khan, S., and Garrido, M., eds. *Connected for Development: Information Kiosks and Sustainability*. New York: UN ICT Task Force. 2003.

Banarjee, A., and Duflo, E. *Poor Economics*. New York: Public Affairs. 2011.

Beardsley, Scott, Moregenstern, Ingo Beyer, and Verbeke, Walter. "Towards a New Regulatory Compact" in *The Global Information Technology Report 2003–04*. 71–86. New York: Oxford University Press. 2004.

Bianchi, P., and Labory, S. *Industrial Policy after the Crisis,* Northampton, MA: Edward Elgar. 2011.

Bresnahan, T.F., and Trajtenberg, M. "General Purpose Technologies: engines of Growth?" *Journal of Econometrics, 65*. 83–108. 1995.

Broadbent, Marianne, and Kitzis, Ellen S. *The New CIO Leader*. Boston: Harvard Business School Press. 2005.

Brownsword, Roger. *Rights, Regulation and the Technological Revolution*. New York: Oxford University Press. 2008.

Brynolfsson, E., and Kahin, B., eds. *Understanding the Digital Economy*. 49–95. Cambridge, MA: MIT Press. 2000.

Brynjolfsson, E., and Saunders, A. *Wired for Innovation: How Information Technology is Reshaping the Economy*. Boston, MA: MIT Press. 2010.

Carr, Nicholas. *Big Switch: Rewiring the World, From Edison to Google*. Boston: Harvard Business School Press. 2008.

Castells, Manuel. *The Information Age: Economy, Society and Culture. Volume I. The Rise of the Network Society*. Malden and Oxford: Blackwell. 1996.

Castells, Manuel, and Cardoso, Gustavo, eds. *The Networked Society: From Knowledge to Policy*. Washington,: Johns Hopkins Center for Transatlantic Relations. 2006.

Cecchini, S., and Scott, C. "Can Information and Communication Technology Applications Contribute to Poverty Reduction: Lessons from Rural India." *Information Technology for Development, Vol. 10*. 73–84. 2003.

Claessens, S., Glaessner, T., and Klingbiel, D. *E-Finance in Emerging Markets: Is Leapfrogging Possible?* Washington, DC: The World Bank. 2001.

Cowhey, P.F., and Aronson, J.D. *Transforming Global Information and Communication Market, the Political Economy of Innovation*. Cambridge MA: MIT Press. 2009.

Davenport, T.H., and Harris, J.G. *Competing on Analytics: The New Science of Winning*. Boston, MA: Harvard Business School Press. 2007.

Davenport, T., and Jarvenpaa, S. *Strategic Use of Analytics in Government*. Washington, DC: IBM Center for the Business of Government. 2008.

Dunleavy, Patrick, Helen Margetts, Simon Bastow, and Jane Tinkler. *Digital Era Governance*. New York: Oxford University Press. 2008.

Dutta, S., and Mia, I., eds. *The Global Information Technology Report 2007–08.* New York: Palgrave MacMillan. 2008.

The Economist. The 2004 e-readiness rankings. London: Economist Intelligence Unit. 2004.

The Economist, TEDGlobal: Cloud schools offer new education. 2013a

The Economist, Why does Kenya lead the world in mobile money. 2013b

Ericsson's Networked Society City Index. 2013. http://www.ericsson.com/res/docs/2013/ns-city-index-report-2013.pdf

Ericsson. *Digital Tech Transforming Industry, Society, and Life.* 2014. http://www.ericsson.com/news/140404-digital-tech-transforming-industry-society-life_244099437_c

Eggers, William. *Government 2.0.* New York: Rowman & Littlefield. 2005.

Eggers, William, and Singh, Shalabh. *The Public Innovator's Playbook: Nurturing bold ideas in government.* Cambridge, MA: Deloitte Research and Ash Institute. 2009.

European Commission. *Smarter, Faster, Better eGovernment: Eighth e-Government Benchmark Measurement.* Brussels: EC. 2009.

European Commission. *Digital Agenda: Turning government data into gold.* Brussels: EC. 2011. http://europa.eu/rapid/press-release_IP-11-1524_en.htm

Foster, C., and Heeks, R. "Innovation and Scaling of ICT for the Bottom-of-the-pyramid," in *Journal of Information Technology,* 28. 296–315. 2013.

Fountain, Jane E. *Building the Virtual State.* Washington: Brookings Institution. 2001.

Friedrich, R., Sabbagh, K., El-Darwiche, B., and Singh, M. "Digital Highways: The Role of Government in 21st Century Infrastructure." Booz & Company. 2009. http://www.strategyand.pwc.com/global/home/what-we-think/reports-white-papers/article-display/digital-highways-role-government-21st

Gelb, Alan, and Decker, Caroline. *Cash at Your Fingertips: Biometric Technology for Transfers in Developing and Resource-Rich Countries.* Working paper 253. Washington, DC: Center for Global Development. 2011.

Gencer, Menekse. "The Mobile Money Movement: Catalyst to Jump-Start Emerging Markets." *Innovations: Technology, Governance, Globalization* 6, no. 1:101–17. 2011.

Gigler, B., and Bailur, S. *Closing the Feedback Loop.* Washington, DC: The World Bank. 2014.

Gupta, P.M., Kumar, Prabhat, and Bhattacharya, Jaijit. *Government Online: Opportunities and Challenges.* New Delhi: Tata McGraw-Hill. 2004.

Gurin, J. *Open Data Now.* McGraw-Hill Education. 2013.

Hanna, Nagy K. *The Information Technology Revolution and Economic Development.* World Bank Discussion paper 120. Washington, DC: The World Bank. 1991.

Hanna, Nagy K., and Boyson, Sandor. *Information Technology in World Bank Lending.* World Bank Discussion Paper, Number 206. Washington, DC: The World Bank. 1993.

Hanna, Nagy K. *Exploiting of Information Technology for Development: A Case Study of India.* World Bank Discussion Paper, Number 246. Washington, DC: The World Bank. 1994.

Hanna, Nagy K., and Picciotto, Robert. *Making Development Work: Development Learning in a World of Wealth and Poverty,* New Jersey: Transactions Publications. 2002.

Hanna, Nagy K. *From Envisioning to Designing e-Development: The Experience of Sri Lanka.* Washington DC: The World Bank. 2007a.

Hanna, Nagy K. *e-Leadership Institutions for the Knowledge Economy.* World Bank Institute Working Paper. Washington, DC: The World Bank, 2007b.

Hanna, Nagy K. *Transforming Government and Empowering Communities: The Experience of Sri Lanka.* Washington, DC: The World Bank. 2008.

Hanna, Nagy K. *e-Transformation: Enabling New Development Strategies.* New York: Springer. 2009. http://www.amazon.com/-Transformation-Development-Strategies-Innovation-Technology/dp/1441978437/ref=sr_1_20?ie=UTF8&qid=1288206653&sr=8-20

Hanna, Nagy K., and Qiang, Christine. "Trends in National E-Government Institutions" in *Information and Communications for Development 2009: Extending Reach and Increasing Impact.* Washington, DC: The World Bank. 2009.

Hanna, Nagy K. *Enabling Enterprise Transformation: Business and Grassroots Innovation for the Knowledge Economy.* New York: Springer. 2010a.

Hanna, Nagy K. *Transforming Government and Building the Information Society: Challenges and Opportunities for the Developing World.* New York: Springer. 2010b. http://www.amazon.com/Transforming-Government-Building-Information-Society/dp/1441978453/ref=sr_1_15?ie=UTF8&qid=1288206618&sr=8-15

Hanna, Nagy K. *Open Development: ICT for Governance in Africa.* Washington, DC: The World Bank. 2012a.

Hanna, Nagy K. *Open, Smart, and Inclusive Development: ICT for Transforming North Africa.* Abidjan: African Development Fund. 2012b.

http://zunia.org/fr/post/open-smart-and-inclusive-development-ict-for-transforming-north-africa

Hanna, Nagy K., and Knight, Peter T. *Seeking Transformation through Information Technology.* New York: Springer. 2011. http://books.google.com/books/about/Seeking_Transformation_Through_Informati.html?id=CkjaLpd-PVYC

Hanna, Nagy K., and Knight, Peter T. *National Strategies to Harness Information Technology: Seeking Transformation in Singapore, Finland, the Philippines, and South Africa.* New York: Springer. 2012. http://books.google.com/books/about/National_Strategies_to_Harness_Informati.html?id=rbVPumrlRyUC

Heeks, Richard. *ICT4D 2.0 Manifesto: Where Next for ICTs and International Development?* Development Informatics, Working Paper Series. Manchester: University of Manchester, Institute for Development Policy and Development. 2009.

Heeks, R. *ICT4D 2016: New Priorities for ICT4D Policy, Practice, and WSIS in a Post-2015 World.* Manchester: Center for Development Informatics,

Institute for Development Policy and Management, University of Manchester. 2014.

Helpman, Elhanan, ed. *General Purpose Technologies and Economic Growth.* Cambridge, MA: MIT Press. 1998.

Hilbert, Martin, and Katz, Jorge. *Building an Information Society: Latin American and Caribbean Perspective.* Santiago: ECLAC. 2003.

Hobsbawm, E.J. *Industry and Empire: from 1750 to the Present Day,* London: Penguin Books. 1969.

http://researchguides.worldbankimflib.org/content.php?pid=44774&sid=331261 — on overall sources for ICT sector for development publications and e-gov resource guide.

http://www.egov4dev.org/links/#main — on e-gov online resources eg, national e-gov strategies sites.

http://www.erepublic.org — links to national government portals worldwide.

http://unpan.org/DPADM/EGovernment/UNEGovernmentSurveys/tabid/600/language/en-US/Default.aspx — on UN e-government surveys and global rankings.

http://www.opengovdata.org on the principles of open government data

http://www.pwc.com/gx/en/psrc/publications/future-of-government.jhtml — on the future of government.

http://www.ida.gov.sg/Collaboration-and-Initiatives/Initiatives/Store/M-Government.aspx Singapore Mobile Gov apps.

https://cio.gov — US Federal CIO council organization, functions, agenda.

IFC. *Mobile Money Study 2011.* Washington, DC. 2011. http://www.ifc.org/wps/wcm/connect/fad057004a052eb88b23ffdd29332b51/MobileMoneyReport-Summary.pdf?MOD=AJPERES

IFC. *Doing Business.* Washington, DC.: World Bank. 2013.

ITU: Measuring the Information Society. Geneva: ITU. 2013a.

http://www.itu.int/en/ITU-D/Statistics/Documents/publications/mis2013/MIS2013_without_Annex_4.pdf

ITU, ICT Success Stories, Geneva: ITU. 2013b. http://www.itu.int/ITU-D/ict_stories/themes/poverty.html

Kelly T., and Rossotto, C. eds. *Broadband Strategies Handbook*. Washington, DC: World Bank. 2012. www.broadband-toolkit.org.

Kendall, Jake, Maurer, Bill, Machoka, Phillip, and Clara Veniard. "An Emerging Platform: From Money Transfer System to Mobile Money Ecosystem." *Innovations: Technology, Governance, Globalization*6, no. 4. 49–65. 2011.

Kettl, Donald, and Kelman, Steven. *Reflections on 21st Century of Government Management*. Washington DC: IBM Center for the Business of Government. 2007.

Knight, Peter T. *The Internet in Brazil: Origins, Strategy, Development, and Governance*. Bloomington: AuthorHouse. 2014.

Kressel, Henry. *Competing for the Future: How Digital Innovations are Changing the World*. New York: Cambridge University Press. 2007.

Labelle, Richard. *ICT Policy Formulation and e-Strategy Development*. UNDP-APDIP Asia Pacific Development Information Programme. New Delhi, India: Elsevier India. 2005.

Lanvin, Bruno, "Leaders and Facilitators: The New Roles of Governments in Digital Economies" in *The Global Information Technology Report 2002-03*. World Economic Forum. Oxford University Press. 2003.

Lipsey, R.G., Carlaw, K.I., and Bekar, C.T. *Economic Transformations*. New York: Oxford University Press. 2005.

Mas, Ignacio, and Kabir Kumar. "Banking on Mobiles: Why, Who and for Whom?" Focus Note 48. Washington, DC: CGAP. 2008.

Mansell, Robin, and When, U., eds. *Knowledge Societies: Information Technology for Sustainable Development*. Oxford: Oxford University Press. 1998.

Mansell, Robin, Avgerou, Chrisanthi, Quah, Danny, and Silverstone, Roger, eds. *The Oxford Handbook of Information and Communications Technologies*. Oxford: Oxford University Press. 2007.

McKinsey Global Institute. *Big Data: The next frontier for innovation, competition, and productivity.* 2011. http://www.mckinsey.com/insights/ business_technology/big_data_the_next_frontier_for_innovation

Melhem, S., Morrell, C., and Tandon, N. *Information and Communications Technologies for Women's Socioeconomic Empowerment.* Washington, DC: World Bank. 2009.

Melody, W.H. "Policy Implications of the New Information Economy," in M. Tool and P. Bush eds. *Institutional Analysis and Economic Policy.* Dordrecht: Kluwer, 411-432. 2003.

Mintzberg, H., Ahlstrand, B., and Lampel, J. *Strategy Safari.* NY: The Free Press. 1998.

Morawczynski, Olga. *Examining the Adoption, Usage and Outcomes of Mobile Money Services. The Case of M-PESA in Kenya.* Edinburgh: University of Edinburgh. 2010. https://www. era.lib.ed.ac.uk/bitstream/1842/5558/2/Morawczynski 2011.pdf

Morawczynski, Olga, and Krepp, Sean. "Saving on the Mobile: Developing Innovative Financial Services to Suit Poor Users," *The Mobile Financial Services Development Report.* 51–58. Washington, DC: World Economic Forum. 2011.

Morgan, Bronwen, ed. *The Intersection of Rights and Regulation.* Hampshire: Ashgate Publishing. 2007.

Muente-Kunigami, A., and Navas-Sabater, J. "Options to Increase Access to Telecommunication Services in Rural and Low-Income Areas." World Bank Working Paper 178, Washington, DC: The World Bank. 2010.

Nambisan, Satish. *Transforming Government Through Collaborative Innovation.* Washington, DC: IBM Center for the Business of Government. 2008.

OECD and ITU. *M-Government: Mobile Technologies for Responsive Governments and Connected Societies.* OECD. 2011. http://dx.doi. org/10.1787/9789264118706-en. OECD. *ICTs and Economic Growth in Developing Countries*. DAC Network on Poverty Reduction. Paris: OECD. 2004a.

OECD. "Lifelong Learning." OECD Policy Brief. Paris: OECD. 2004b.

OECD. *e-Government for Better Government*. Paris: OECD. 2005.

OECD. *Participative Web and User-Created Content: Web 2.0, Wikis, and Social Networking*. Paris: OECD. 2007.

Ogus, A.L. Regulation: Legal Form and Economic Theory. Oxford: Oxford University Press. 1994.

Qiang, Christine Z., and Rosotto, Carlo. "Economic Impact of Broadband" in *2009 Information and Communication for Development: Extending Reach and Increasing Impact*. Washington DC: World Bank. 2009.

Paltridge, Sam. "User-driven innovation and communications development" in Chandra, V. Erocal, D., Padoan, P., and Braga, C. eds. *Innovation and Growth*. Paris: OECD. 2009.

Perez, Carlota. *Technological Revolutions and Financial Capital*. Cheltenham: Edward Elgar. 2002.

Prahalad, C. K. *The Fortune at the Bottom of the Pyramid*. New Jersey: Wharton School Publishing. 2005.

Prosser, T. The Limits of Competition Law: Markets and Public Services. Oxford: Oxford University Press, 2005.

Prosser, T. *The Regulatory Enterprise*. New York: Oxford University Press. 2010.

Ramsey, Todd. *On Demand Government: Continuing the E-government Journey*. Indiana: IBM Press. 2004.

Rodrik, Dani. 2007. *One Economics, Many Recipes*. Princeton: Princeton University.

Rubino-Hallman, Silvana, and Hanna, Nagy K. "New Technologies for Public Sector Transformation: A Critical Analysis of e-Government Initiatives in Latin America and the Caribbean." *Journal for e-Government* 3 (3): 3–39. 2006

Sachs, J. "The Digital War on Poverty." *The Guardian*, August 21. 2008.

Saylor, Michael. *The Mobile Wave*. Boston: Da Capo Press. 2013.

Shapiro, Carl, and Varian, Hal R. *Information Rules: A Strategic guide to the Network Economy.* Boston: Harvard Business School Press. 1999.

Spence, Michael. *The Next Convergence.* New York: Farrar, Straus and Giroux. 2011.

Suh, J., Chen, D.H.C. *Korea as a Knowledge Economy: Evolutionary Process and Lessons Learned.* Washington DC: World Bank. 2007.

Stauffacher, D., Hattotuwa, D., and Weekes, B. *The Potential and Challenges of Open Data for Crisis Information Management and Aid Efficiency: A Preliminary Assessment.* ICT4Peace Foundation, 2012.

Stiglitz, Joseph. "Towards a New Paradigm for Development: Strategies, Policies, and Processes," Ninth Raul Prebisch Lecture, United Nations Conference on Trade and Development, delivered at the Palais des Nations, Geneva. October 19. 1998.

Sunstein, C.R. After the Rights Revolution—Reconceiving the Regulatory State. Cambridge: Harvard University Press. 1990.

Turcano, Michael. Knowledge Maps: ICT in Education. Washington, DC: infoDev/World Bank. 2005.

UK e-government strategy. 2011 https://www.gov.uk/government/ publications/uk-govrnment-ict-strategy-resources

UNCTAD. *Information Economy Report 2010.* New York, Geneva: UNCTAD. 2010.

United Nations. *E-government survey: Towards a More Citizen-Centric Approach.* New York: Department of Economic and Social Affairs. 2011. http://unpan1.un.org/intradoc/groups/public/documents/un/ unpan047965.pdf

United Nations. High-level Panel on the Post-2015 Development Agenda. New York: UN. 2013. http://www.post2015hlp.org/ the-report/

UNDP. Egypt: Smart School Network. 2007. http://web.undp.org/com-toolkit/success-stories/ARAB-Egypt-povred2.shtml

UNESCO. *Media and Good Governance.* Paris: UNESCO. 2005.

West, Darrell M. *Digital Government: Technology and Public Sector Performance.* Princeton: Princeton University Press. 2005.

Weatherill, S. ed. *Better Regulation.* Oxford: Hart Publishing. 2007.

Wilson, Ernest J., III. *The Information Revolution and Developing Countries.* Cambridge: MIT Press. 2004.

World Bank. *Knowledge for Development, World Development Report 1998–99.* Washington, DC: The World Bank. 1999.

World Bank. *Making Services Work for Poor People. World Development Report 2004.* Washington, DC: The World Bank and Oxford University Press. 2004.

World Bank. *E-development: From Excitement to Effectiveness.* Global Information and Communication Technologies Department. Washington, DC: The World Bank. 2005.

World Bank on ICT 2013 country indicators /benchmarking http://data.worldbank.org/products/data-books/little-data-book-on-info-communication-tech

World Bank. http://data.worldbank.org/about/open-government-data-toolkit/readiness-assessment-tool

World Bank. *Information and Communications for Development 2006. Global Trends and Policies.* Washington, DC: The World Bank. 2006

World Bank. *To Give People Voice: Media and Broadcasting Development.* Washington, DC: The World Bank. 2007.

World Bank. *Information and Communications for Development 2009. Extending Reach and Increasing Impact.* Washington, DC: The World Bank. 2009.

World Bank. Transformation-Ready: The strategic application of ICT in Africa (Education). 2011a.

World Bank/infoDev/IFC/ITU. *Telecommunications Regulation Handbook.* 2011b. http://www.infodev.org/articles/10th-anniversary-telecommunications-regulation-handbook

World Bank. *Maximizing Mobile.* Washington DC: The World Bank. 2012.

World Bank and African Development Bank. *eTransform Africa.* 2012. www.etransformafrica.org.

World Economic Forum. *The Future of Government: Lessons Learned from around the World.* 2011a. http://www.weforum.org/news/future-government-lessons-learned-around-world

World Economic Forum. *Mobile Financial Services Development Report.* 2011b. http://www.weforum.org/issues/mobile-financial-services-development.

World Economic Forum. *Big Data, Big Impact: New Possibilities for International Development.* 2012. http://www.weforum.org/reports/big-data-big-impact-new-possibilities-international-development

The Authors

———

Dr. Nagy K. Hanna is an author, educator, public speaker, and global expert on digital transformation and innovation strategies. He is an adviser to governments, ICT multinationals, and major consulting firms on cutting-edge ICT policies and strategies. He has forty years of experience advising countries and aid agencies on digital economy, e-transformation policies and strategies, e-government, e-leadership institutions, knowledge services industry, public-sector reform and governance, and innovation-driven development strategies. He is a senior fellow and board member of the Center for Policy on Emerging Technologies; member of editorial boards of several journals, including *Springer's* and *Palgrave's*, and their book series on Innovation, Entrepreneurship, Technology and Knowledge Economy. He has taught at several universities and led or participated in development policy dialogue in over fifty countries. Published over one hundred papers and book chapters, and authored or coauthored twenty books. Over thirty years, he held many positions at the World Bank, including senior adviser on national ICT strategies, lead evaluator of development effectiveness, lead corporate strategist, lead economist, and senior operations officer. He holds a PhD from Wharton School, University of Pennsylvania, and an executive development diploma from Harvard. nagyhanna@comcast.net

Rene Summer is a director of government and industry relations at Ericsson Group with global responsibility for national ICT strategy, media/content regulation, copyright, media convergence, and data protection. Within these policy areas, he is responsible for conducting strategic business impact assessments (SWOT), policy research, policy formulation, and advocacy. He contributes with his expertise to Ericsson's corporate technology office and strategy planning office and Ericsson's business unit's strategic business planning, Ericsson's central and local offices. He has been on the board of Internet Industry Association of Australia and is an active member of different working groups of various industry associations. He has also been appointed by a number of government authorities as special adviser to advise special working groups and committees. He holds an MSc degree from Reading University in the United Kingdom in International Business and Finance. rene.summer@ericsson.com

www.ingramcontent.com/pod-product-compliance
Lightning Source LLC
Chambersburg PA
CBHW050506210326
41521CB00011B/2347